FOR YOU

A GUIDE FROM THE UNIVERSE

Deborah Hales

Cover image courtesy of European Space Agency/Hubble.

Copyright © 2020 by Deborah Hales

All rights reserved. No part of this publication may be reproduced, distributed, or transmitted in any form or by any means, including photocopying, recording, or other electronic or mechanical methods, without the prior written permission of the publisher, except in the case of brief quotations embodied in critical reviews and certain other noncommercial uses permitted by copyright law.

ISBN 978-1-6588173-0-1

First Edition

Printed in the United States of America

Table of Contents

Foreword v

Our Introduction vii

Who You Are 9

Who Created You 33

The Plan of Happiness 43

Your Place in the Plan 71

The Laws and Truths We Function Within 85

How to See and Recognize Truth 93

The Lies 123

Steps to Take to Return Home 143

Who Are You Now? 163

What Do You Do Now? 171

Foreword

The journey I have been privileged to travel, to bring this book to the world, has taken me to unexpected places, introduced me to precious souls, enlightened my understanding, and touched my heart in ways I could never before have imagined. Those that have shared their stories and thoughts have done so with you in mind.

My greatest hope is that you will understand how much you are loved, your heart will be filled with hope and peace, your mind will be enlightened, and you will recognize the messages in these pages that were meant just *for you*.

Deborah Hales

Our Introduction

The timeless words on the pages that follow are ancient. They will speak to the parts of you that are just as old. You will feel a stirring in the deep places of who you truly are. Don't be alarmed. Let the awareness and the remembering happen. There will be room on some of the pages, set aside throughout the book, for you to write down your feelings, ideas, or thoughts that come to you. To receive what this book was written to accomplish clear your mind, open your heart and get ready to welcome the truths you will recognize.

Peltau

There will be moments as you read that you will feel drawn into the truths contained therein and there will be other moments when you have to close the book and walk away.

But please come back.

Samson

This book was written for you. Think of it as a manual, a workbook, a best friend, a sounding board, a therapist, a place to go to find the answers to the questions your soul, your essence, your energy has been searching for, for as long as you can remember. Find a quiet place to drink from its pages. Your thirst for answers will be rewarded as the truths you are seeking will come to you.

Trevor

CHAPTER 1

Who You Are

There was a moment in your life when you started to question why you are here. Up to that point you didn't question. You inherently knew you have a place and a purpose here.

When you began to question, to see, and to wonder, you opened yourself up to answers from a variety of sources: some positive and building sources and some negative and degrading sources.

As you begin our journey of remembering why you are here, inklings of truth will start to present themselves. Thoughts, feelings, phrases, words that fit, that feel right, will start to light up your senses, your heart, and your mind. As you give these thoughts, feelings, phrases and words space to grow, more remembering will occur.

At the same time, due to the law of polarity, which states that everything of consequence has an opposite, inklings of untruths will make their way into your thoughts, feelings, words and phrases.

The forces of darkness don't want you to succeed here in this earth life. But, the forces of light are more powerful than the forces of darkness and ultimately the forces of light will succeed.

Because of your innocence and impressionability as a child you listened to all of it, and so began the conflict of who you truly are.

Albert

Everything has a time and a season. This is the time for you to remember who you are. You have been told who you are by family, friends, acquaintances, partners, clergy, and even your reflection in the mirror.

Complete this statement with words that you feel describe you:
I am _____
I am _____
I am _____
I am _____

Once you have written down all the "I am" statements, look over them. Read each one and feel your reaction. Cross out the ones you know aren't true. Look at the list again. Read each one of the statements. How did it make you feel?

Write down the "I am" statements that you want to be true about you:
I am_____
I am_____
I am_____
I am_____

Who You Are

Sit with these statements individually. Eliminate the ones that don't feel right. Once you have the "I am" statements you want to be true, that feel right to you, say them out loud as often as possible and watch the miracles come to you.

Raymond

As a boy I questioned everything. The world was a place of wonder. So many things to explore and experiment with and upon. My mother was a very smart woman and could answer most of my questions. The ones she couldn't answer were the ones about who we are. She apologized, "It is just how things are. Some questions weren't meant to be answered." I couldn't accept that and continued to ponder about who we are.

I never gave up wanting to know who I was beyond my family, and life went on. One day, in a quiet moment, I was taken in my mind to a place where there were many people. It was a peaceful but busy place. Everyone seemed to have something important to do. I stopped one of the people and asked them where I was. They smiled and pointed to an elderly gentleman. He looked up and by the look on his face I knew he knew why I was there.

He put down what he was doing and threw his arms around me calling me by name. It felt as if we had known each other. I would come to find out that we did. He led me to an overlook that looked out over a massive expanse. It became clear that when an earthly body was conceived a signal or connection was activated in the spirit body that would inhabit that particular physical body.

The physical body would be formed using the spirit body as a template. There was a lot of excitement associated with their impending trip to earth. It looked like the spirit bodies that had been "activated" had many other spirits that loved and cared about them. They were excited as well as sad. The sadness was because of the separation that would occur once those spirits left that realm and all who loved them and began their existence on earth.

My eyes were drawn to a group of spirits who seemed to be gathering. Another being approached them who was different than the others. Glorious and brilliant. As He conversed with them, I could hear them call him Father. Before I knew it, He was looking at me and calling me by name. In that moment I knew He was my Father too. When I came to myself, I knew my question was being answered. Now I wanted to know about my Father.

Cerano

You are part of a vast network that includes everything. You most likely will not feel the death of an ant that is stepped on by an unsuspecting person, but the ant's death changed things. You are of more consequence than the ant. Therefore, more things change when you are removed from this earthly existence.

Find something in nature that you can sit with for a bit. If you picked a tree, for instance, observe the tree. Focus on it. Notice the leaves, the colors, the bark, the placement of each limb, where it enters the ground. Are there any nests? Are there any scars on the trunk or limbs? Does it seem old or young? Healthy or sick?

Write your observations down on the space below. Take as long as you want.

Who You Are

_____
_____
_____
_____

Whatever you chose to focus on has always been there. You just haven't taken the time to be still and quiet with it. You may have felt gratitude for it without even trying.

You might try this exercise with a person or an animal or anything really. See what happens and record your thoughts.

_____
_____
_____
_____

This ability to see something, truly see it, will be important to do later on in the book.

Ronald

Sometime during the earth's existence there was a transformation of great importance. The transformation, when completed, made it possible for life to not only exist, but to thrive.

To support life, the elements of the earth and of our bodies had to support each other. The air you would breathe needed to be a specific mixture. You are literally part of this earth. Because of this you are connected to this earth at an elemental level. Matter can neither be created or made, it has always existed. That makes the elements of your body ancient, maybe older than ancient. Does that make you timeless like the matter you are made from?

Because your body is not only subject to life but to death as well, you have the ability to connect to what it is your body requires for life.

Jeremy

To prepare for this earth life your spirit was taught, trained and informed, in an outline sort of way, about what your challenges would be and what characteristics you would require to be successful during your experience on earth.

Spirit teachers, mentors, specialists and others were there to help you know how to prepare for these challenges. There was discussion about what character traits you would need for each challenge you would face while on earth. Specific people would be present in your life to help with your challenges. Knowledge and inspiration would come to you as you needed it and asked for it. Your circumstances would give you the opportunity to ask for help, for strength, for inspiration, or not.

The principle of agency has always been in play. You can choose to act or be acted upon. There will be times that other people, exercising their agency, will impact you and your ability to have a choice. But even in that circumstance you will still have choices to make as a result of their choices.

Because your Heavenly Father, or the father of your spirit, wants you to succeed He made sure you would be equipped with the tools necessary for you to do just that. With all the planning, the learning, the support, and the love you gathered during your stay in the world of spirits, you were ready to join your mortal body, with joyful anticipation.

Destiny

Your connection to your mortal body began at conception. Your spiritual body acted as a template for your mortal body to be patterned after as it developed and grew in your mother's womb.

Through your parents and their parents and so on, you inherited physical characteristics, emotional sensitivities and mental tendencies. It is your body and you have the ability to know what's going on when things are out of balance.

Felicity

There have been times in my life when I was so sure about who I was and where I was going that nothing could stop me from accomplishing everything that my heart desired. And shortly after those "nothing could stop me" times came the doubts and the "reality" that I was no one, not important enough to bring forward those things that were burning so brightly in my heart and soul.

What burns brightly in your soul?

_____

_____

FOR YOU: A Guide to the Universe

Sherrie

My dog can see who I am. He knows me better than anyone. I can see in his eyes that I am loved and lovable. When I was sad or had a bad day, he knew just where to position himself: next to my leg, by my side on the couch, or laying ever so softly on one of my feet.

Dogs know who they are. Why can't we be more like dogs?

Spencer

My mom used to say:
> "I know who you are.
> God knows who you are.
> Make us proud."

Then she would squeeze me real tight with a kiss and an "I love you" as I went out the door each day. When I was small, I didn't question what she said. I just knew she knew, and God knew and that meant I knew, of course.

"What did we know?" you might be wondering?

I knew I was worth more than I could imagine. My soul skipped through each day because I knew He was aware of me. He loved me. He knew who I really was and so did my mom. They could see through all the false identities I tried on each day. I was still under there and they helped me shake the false ones off.

Who You Are

Sometimes I wanted to keep them and other times I couldn't get them off fast enough.

I knew who I was but sometimes I forgot, when a boy on my bus told me I was uglier than his dog. I forgot when I tried something hard and failed. I forgot when my best friend became someone else's best friend and pretended she didn't know me.

I forgot, when my boss fired me, and I didn't know how I would pay rent. I forgot, when my husband told me he didn't love me anymore.

Each time I forgot, somewhere, somehow, through darkness and rejection the words Mom would say came into my mind:

"I know who you are.

God knows who you are.

Make us proud."

I made them proud by seeing my beauty through God's and my mother's eyes. By trying again and by loving my best friend anyway. (Side note: we ended up being roommates at college and are best friends still.) I made then proud by thanking the boss that fired me because I ended up finding the best job ever in enough time to pay my rent. I made them proud when I remembered my worth was truly more than I had ever imagined, as I glimpsed myself as God and my mother saw me.

I held onto that glimpse. I cherished that glimpse. That glimpse has gotten me through many times when I thought I had lost it.

What was the glimpse that you saw just now? Did you see it or feel it?

Draw or write it down here.

_____

_____

_____

Stephanie

I saw your day. How disconnected you are from your true selves. How do I know you are disconnected? Your lights are dull. Some are even flickering. You picked up this book because you were drawn to it like a moth to a flame. The truths found within will stop the flickering of your light. They will brighten your light to a blazing, glorious, powerful flame if you put into practice what you will learn. Look for the sparks.

Underline them.

Circle them.

Highlight them.

They will become part of you. We need your light and your brightness. We need you!

Harold

You are a fantastic creature. Inside of you is your authentic, true self just waiting to be set free. Free from all that isn't you. Free from all the chains and the bindings that are your false self and your false identities. All that you have gathered since you came to this earth that isn't serving you.

There have been times in your life where your behavior didn't feel right to you in certain instances. You weren't comfortable with what you said or did, or the choices you made, but you couldn't put your finger on what wasn't right about it.

You might think it was what your parents and/or family taught you about right or wrong, your cultural expectations, your built-in moral compass, and it could be some of all the above.

When you aren't true to yourself, who you truly are, you feel off, maybe confused and frustrated, as to why you can't put your finger on just what is off.

Pause for a minute or two and think of a time you felt like that and record below what comes to your mind.

_____

_____

_____

_____

Have you ever been the one that didn't get picked for something? It was as if no one could see you no matter how much you waved your arms and jumped up and down? That is what your true authentic "you" is doing. Wanting to be seen by you. Wanting to be free to be who you were always meant to be. Waiting for you to notice and waiting for you to have the desire to set who you truly are free. Take a moment and connect to who you truly are; that self that is you with nothing false or unnecessary.

Write down what you hear or feel or see.

_____

_____

Cindy

We had been battling the French for days. Dead bodies lay where they fell. We were completely and utterly exhausted. I was wounded and had lost a lot of blood. I was in and out of what felt like a dream. All across the battlefield there were angels. Some were embracing the spirits of the dead and then leaving with them. Other angels were attending to the dying and to the wounded, of which I was one. I sensed a spirit tending to my injuries in a most delicate manner. It was most comforting. I felt such peace as I drifted in and out of consciousness. As the battle waned some medics found me, and I was taken to the hospital tent. The angel that was with me followed. As I was being treated, she was working alongside the doctors and nurses.

When I woke the next day, bandaged and in pain I could see my angel and many others, helping the doctors and nurses. She smiled at me and was gone. I have kept that experience close to my heart for a couple of reasons. One, I didn't think anyone would believe me and I wasn't confident that it wasn't what was seen by a delirious, battle crazed soldier.

With my eyes shut I can still see so vividly how my angel confidently, yet delicately, reached her hand into my leg. I could see the blood vessels being repaired as if my skin was transparent. She never spoke but her presence filled me with the knowing that God had sent her. That He knew who I was and that it was not my time to go. Because I observed the angels with the spirits of those whose time it was to go, to leave this earthly existence, I was comforted. I saw the tender care that was given them and the peace that finally surrounded them. Such a contrast from the war we were fighting.

There was the spirit of one soldier that I remembered seeing who was very agitated, very angry and would not go with the angels who came for him. They eventually left without him. He continued to remain close to his body, ranting and raving and throwing his arms around in the air. I didn't know him but wished he would have gone with the angels that came for him.

I have always been grateful for that angel who helped repair my physical body so the medics could do their work. I never got to say thank you until now.

Winthrop

It was a rainy night. The smell in the air held a portent of what was coming. I didn't know that my life would change forever in just two short days.

My life to that point had been mediocre, average, nothing exciting or monumental. I was quite satisfied with my lot in life and was content to spend the rest of my life that way.

It was in the morning two days later, that she entered my life. I worked in a medical facility and was introduced to a woman that had been contracted to work with terminally ill patients. I was to accompany her as she visited the patients she had been scheduled to see that day. With each patient she would introduce herself, reach to gently touch them, and then sit with them for different amounts of time. Some were aware of her and others were not.

Each time she would come to the facility I was assigned to accompany her. In the beginning I wasn't sure just what she was doing. As I spent another day following her to another patient and another, I noticed her head bowed in what looked like prayer. It seemed the patient's bodies would gently and easily relax while she was by their side.

One day in the hall she was crying and, when I asked, she told me she sorrows for the pain and suffering she sees they have carried with them. The pain and suffering that has been the cause of their physical diseases or conditions. Then she wiped her tears, regained her composure, and went in to see the next patient on the schedule.

As time went on, I gathered the courage to ask if she would look at my body and see anything I could change to avoid the pain and suffering she was noticing in these patients. She told me to come early the next day and she would see what she could see.

I was a pretty healthy guy and what she told me shocked me. For many years I had had a strained relationship with my father. She told me that the energy of that strained relationship was being held in my left kidney with a connection to my heart. She could already see signs of heart disease beginning to manifest in and around my heart and the energy of the left kidney was fading.

She sensed I was wondering how she could see these things, what they looked like to her, who she really was, and what was she doing with these patients. She explained she had been gifted to be able to see colors and feelings and stories and was there to help heal the spirits of those who would soon be crossing to the other side.

We talked. Well, she listened as I mostly talked about my dad and his story. It became clear to me if I didn't do something to heal this relationship, I would start physically feeling the consequences. With her help I talked with my dad and got the help we needed to heal our relationship, which cascaded to healing our family and others.

She was right about the connection. My kidney perked up and my heart disease diminished.

Bartholomew

You are one of a kind. No one has ever lived or will live, that is like you. Your uniqueness means no one can do "it" like you will do "it." "It" could be how you treat others or how you conduct yourself in general or the words you use to express yourself.

We all, at some time or other, wonder at our beginnings. We wonder about where we came from, where we are, and where we are going. Fear may creep into your thoughts as you ponder on these things, either because you don't know or don't want to know. Is it even possible to know these things? Do we need to know these things?

This earth life is full of connections. One of the most important connections is that of family. Being connected makes us stronger. Being disconnected makes us weaker. Sometimes connections are broken, and alternative connections are made.

What does family mean to you?

_____

_____

_____

_____

Emotionally you can disconnect from your family, but the fact is your family runs in your blood. That connection will never be broken. Other connections may be added to it, but your family will always remain with you.

Do you have strong healthy connections in your family, as you define it? Or disconnections that weaken your foundation?

_____
_____
_____

For a moment, take a step back and look at both sides of the connection, the relationship or lack of one. No matter what they did to you, forgiveness is what will clean up the connections and enable the truth and healing to come in. What would you like your strong and healthy connections to look like?

Describe them below:

_____
_____
_____

Draw on the strengths passed down to you through the generations beginning with Mother Eve and Father Adam. Their blood runs through your veins. Forgive those who passed on belief systems that affected you in a negative way.

Express gratitude for them and their lives and feel the negative influence leave you on all levels of your existence. As you heal and strengthen those connections for yourself, the effects will ripple through your generations.

_____
_____
_____
_____

Samson

I am so excited for you. You have this book. You opened its pages and here we are.

You are made of stardust. Think about it. Your body is made of matter, so is everything in the universe. Your stardust is organized or activated for a time, while you are on earth. What activates the earthly stardust is finer stardust. Earthly matter has a slower vibration which makes it denser. Spirit matter has a higher vibration which makes it finer.

This book, the one you are holding in your hands, is made of both earthly and spirit matter. One you can see, the other you can feel. You were drawn to this book like a moth to a flame. Your spirit matter, your stardust, brought you here. In these pages you will find light and truth. This light and truth might be packaged in a way that you aren't used to, but if you look with your spiritual eyes you will "see" all the treasures this book contains.

The treasures were written *for you.* You have a unique perspective in the way you gather information and process it through all your life experiences, your family patterns, and your own fears and other emotions. How you see the words on this page will be different than the next person. But that is because you will see what you need to see to allow more light and life into your life. Don't judge what insight and "aha"s come into your mind while you read. Write them down. Some will be new ideas and you may forget them if you don't record what comes to you. You will receive as much as you allow yourself to so get ready for some juicy stuff to come your way. It is packaged just *for you*; exactly how you need it to be for you to come to know who you are and what you are here on this earth to do. We are "rooting" for you. You can do this!

Palouse

Next time you are in a group of people look around and observe them one at a time. Really see them. They are you.

Let me explain. One of the people you are observing appears to be worried or concerned about something. He or she is quietly contemplating something important to them. Someone may interact with him or her for a moment and they smile and respond but then they go back to their worries and concerns. You have been where they are so you can relate. They are you.

Another person you observe must be in love. They won't stop smiling. Their face is lit up and they are talking in an animated way to the person they are obviously in love with. They are you.

As you look around and really truly see them, you will connect with them because they are you as you have been before. If you want to take it a bit further, what would have helped you the most when you were worried or concerned about something? Did you need someone to fix it or someone to help you know that everything would work out for your good?

Who You Are

We go through life thinking everyone is so different from us when, in reality, we are more similar than we are different. Our cultures, our languages, our dress and our circumstances may be very different, but when we look into someone else's eyes, we are them and they are us. So, seeing them, truly seeing them, humbles us and makes all of us stronger.

Sala

There was a girl I knew who could see right through me. She could see the truth about me. There was nothing I could hide from her. It really bothered me for a very long time but eventually, I counted on that from her. It was where I had no choice but to be myself. There were no pretenses with her. Do you know anyone like that? Someone who sees through all the fake personas that you think you need to put on.

Sometimes it felt so uncomfortable to be with her because I was trying so hard to be something I wasn't, but that I thought I wanted to be. I wasn't very good at faking it. I was always reminded of the person she could see. Eventually, I gave up on all the fakeness and embraced the person she saw, with all my faults and strengths. I will forever be grateful for her and her ability to see the real me and that she wasn't afraid to tell me the truth, until I could see it too.

Perry

We are fragile beings as we navigate through this earthly experience until who we truly are emerges. The fragility comes from our doubts, our fears and our confusion. So, what do you do? Live a miserable life filled with doubt, fear and confusion? Or do you exchange the negative emotions for positive ones? How do I do that you might ask? This will take some work on your part. Are you willing to put in some effort? If so, let's get started.

We need to establish a few truths before we begin:

1. You can know stuff about you. All you have to do is ask the right questions.

2. You have the ability to change matter. Your brain is made up of matter. Your thoughts and emotions create chemical changes in your body. Chemicals are matter. You can change your thoughts. You don't have to understand how it all works to be able to make these changes. You only have to believe.

3. No matter what your circumstances have been up to this point, YOU CAN CHANGE YOUR FUTURE.

The template below is something you can use over and over again by inserting one thing you don't like and want to change. Then ponder the questions that follow and write down your answers.

Write down one thing you hate about yourself:

_____
_____
_____

1. Why does this bother me so much? Why do I feel strongly about it?

_____

Who You Are

_____
_____
_____

2. Get very quiet and ponder about how you want to feel. Write what came to you as you pondered:

_____
_____
_____
_____

3. For a moment, imagine yourself the way you want to be. Feel how you feel more like yourself, true to who you really are. Sit with that for a bit. Connect with your true self, with all your parts and pieces present and working together.

Write down what you are experiencing:

_____
_____
_____
_____

4. You just changed your matter. You are more powerful than you know.

Record what comes to you:
_____
_____
_____
_____

To please everyone, pieces of you get scattered, when what they really need is for to be your authentic, amazing, strong, and powerful self.

5. Try on this "new" self you have rediscovered, live in it for a bit. Be aware of how the world looks a bit different since you did this exercise. It looks different because you are seeing it with new eyes. It will feel right because these new eyes are the eyes you have always had. Hold onto this authentic part of you that you have just reconnected with. Allow it to permeate every cell of your body and spirit.

Record what you experience:
_____
_____
_____
_____

Landau

On this journey of discovering and reconnecting with who you truly are, remember this one thing. You were prepared before you came to earth to succeed. You came here with a purpose that only you can fulfill. You will one day account for what you did or did not do. That being said, everything you need to succeed is here as well, whether it be in the form of other people, the written, heard or spoken word, inspiration or unexpected places. So, with eyes wide open, expect to be supported, guided and successful in

Who You Are

accomplishing the reasons you came here to this beautiful, completely messy, wonderful place.

Beatrice

You are a being of light. You can feel, and others can see when your light is on. You can also feel when your light dims and others can see that too. When your light shines brightly life seems good. You can think more clearly. You have the energy to notice someone else's needs and can help them. You tend to think positively when your light is bright.

On the other hand, when your light dims because of doubt, anger, illness, discouragement, bad news or a myriad of other things, your energy diminishes. You think more negatively, and you tend to think more about yourself and not others.

Living with your light dimmed is an uncomfortable way to live. Life seems harder to do. A dim light seems to open you up to more dimness and more negativity. So how do you increase your light and get yourself back to a positive energetic place?

The first step is to be aware of what made your light dim. If you are sick, follow the steps to support your body in its healing process. If it was bad news be hopeful that everything will be okay. You can use these ideas to boost your light:

1. Find a positive "I am" statement to counteract the negative state you are in.
2. Listen to music that makes you happy.
3. Do something nice for someone else.
4. Ask for guidance, pray
5. Be out in nature.
6. Do something that brings you joy.

7. Color out the negative feelings.
8. Drink enough water.
9. Choose the light.
10. Breathe

Remember what works best to get your light shining brightly and the next time it starts to dim do that thing and your light won't be dim for long.

Cindy

CHAPTER 2

Who Created You

There is a point of creation where each of you came into being. The creative process began long before that. Your spirit body was created by your Heavenly Mother and your Heavenly Father. An earth was prepared to form your physical bodies. Your spirit body served as a template for your physical body to be formed from.

Albert

You were created by Gods who love you and who want to share with you all they are and all they have. This may go contrary to what you have been taught. If it does, try to find a place in your heart and mind to ask whether this is the truth or not. Be still and wait for a feeling or a thought.

Write what you felt or heard.

_____

_____

You were created for your progression but also to help others progress. The Gods love you; they know you by name. You knew them before you came to this earth and you will know them when you return to the world of spirits. Before you came to earth, they taught you. They walked with you. They helped you receive all you would need to be successful here. Successful in doing what you needed to do here in order to return to live with them again and continue to progress. You can communicate with them now and continue to learn and progress with their guidance and direction. You are never, ever alone.

Chase

I had a dream that I was in heaven before I came to earth. I was in a most beautiful and peaceful place. I was walking through a beautiful garden with a man who was my friend. I felt strongly the love we had for each other. We talked about my upcoming birth and some things I would need to be prepared for. We discussed how I would need to act and what the consequences would be.

As we walked and talked, others joined us here and there as if on cue to let me know they would be there for me. Others came to share their gifts with me and to talk about their experiences. So much love abounded in this place. I remember feeling so much strength from everyone there. I felt like I could do anything.

Who Created You

My friend was by my side the whole time while all the others came and went. He seemed to know me better than any of the others. He had me look into his eyes and asked me to tell him what I saw. I looked intently into his eyes and felt the greatest love I've ever felt wash over me from my head to my toes. It filled me.

I held my gaze because I felt like there was more I needed to know. In a moment, I knew. I knew He would be right there with me through my experience on earth. He was my friend, a friend like no other I would ever know or have. The one that would be there no matter what I did or thought and no matter what anyone else did or thought. I memorized that moment so I would never forget the feelings I was experiencing.

When I awoke from my dream, I couldn't stop the tears. I was overwhelmed with hope and love and peace and happiness. I had forgotten all of this and life had become so hard for me. What a gift the dream was because I remembered. So when I start to worry or doubt or become confused, I close my eyes and I remember.

Candice

He who is our father is also our creator. He is kind. He is fair. He is wise. He loves us. He cherishes us. He thinks about us. He is aware of us. He is indulging of us. He is grateful for us. He teaches us. He prepares us. He respects us. He wants us to succeed. He is order. He is with us. He respects our decisions. Each of us is precious to him.

Jose

If I were to say to you that a God had created you, what would be your reaction? Would you be curious or reject the idea completely? If you are open to the idea that God created you, you might want to know who this God is.

He is the father of your spirit. He knows you. He believes in you. He respects your ability to choose what you want to do, to be, and to accomplish. He is your greatest cheerleader. He wants only what is best for you. He is always accessible to you. You know Him because you knew Him before you came to this earth.

James

I am grateful for every breath He lends me. For every day I have to grow and do better. Have you ever heard of the saying, "I brought you into this world, I can take you out"? In God's case it is true, He holds that power. It humbles me to a place of gratitude and understanding that I am not in charge. What I am in charge of is my choices while I have breath in me.

We are creators too. As we build a structure, use a recipe and make something delicious to eat, or "make" a child, we get a glimpse into what gods can do and have done and are doing. I have been told I can become a god. So, I must be a god in the making.

How do you feel about that?

Who Created You

Sandy

★ ✹ ★

I have a story to tell. It happened long, long ago. I was privileged to know a god. But he didn't start out that way.

I became aware of a man who was doing miraculous things. Out of curiosity I went one day to where people were gathering. He had healed a blind man and word spread quickly. Many people were there. I had my mother with me. People brought many who were invalid or were suffering. I was captivated as I watched him. He was gentle and kind. There were other men around him who seemed protective and who seemed to love him deeply.

There was something about him that drew me to him. I don't know how long I remained in the crowd of people who gathered but I realized it was the cool of the evening and people were dispersing. It was then that his eyes met mine. A warmth spread through me and my heart seemed to melt. No words were said.

I felt to ask if they needed a meal or a place to lodge for the night. After some discussion they agreed to follow us home.

After they were fed and comfortable, I approached the man named Jesus with a question.

Who are you? My question came from a desire to know why I had the feelings I did when he looked at me earlier. As I sat and listened to him that night, something stirred in me more powerful than anything I could have imagined. It seemed his words were meant just for me. Every question, every concern, and every doubt seemed to be satisfied, resolved, and put behind me as if they never existed.

It was as if my world had changed, but I knew it was something in me that had changed. Every chance I got I watched and listened to him preach, teach and heal. I was the recipient of his healing touch after I severely burned my hand. Some evenings he and his disciples would lodge at my house. Even in his weariness he took time to share with us the truths of the gospel and who we are.

My heart broke during his trial and his crucifixion. But what joy we all experienced when we found out he lived. I got to see him briefly before he left us for good. Words can't express the joy and love I felt when I saw him and witnessed him resurrected.

What I know to be true:

1. Jesus Christ is my Savior and Redeemer. Through Him I can return to live with God again.

2. He and God the Father created this world and our bodies.

3. Jesus Christ is our example of how we can progress to become a God like Him and His Father.

4. He knows me, and He knows you.

5. He is real.

6. He lives.

Susannah

Since the beginning of time people have wondered about where they came from and how they got here. I too wondered about the same thing. There were many around me who had their own opinions on the subject but none of them seemed right to me.

One day I was making bread and assembling the ingredients, my mind became very aware of each ingredient: the flour, the water, the salt, the oil and the leavening agent. While mixing the flour, water, salt and oil together I was very aware of each separate ingredient and I, as the "creator," had chosen each one for a reason. Their quality was important to me because I wanted a delicious and beautiful loaf of bread in the end. The leavening I chose for the flavor it would bring to the bread. The combination of the flour, water, salt, and oil was like the body and the leavening was like the spirit. It brought the bread mixture to life, and I was the creator. It seemed such a simple analogy, but it allowed me to have a glimpse into the principle my creator used to create me.

I see other examples of creators using this principle to create beautiful, useful, magnificent things and am reminded of my creator. There is a huge gap between creating a loaf of bread and creating a body, but the principle is universal.

He, our creator, is real. We are created with love. Love is the magical ingredient that makes the bread taste so good. Our creator's love for us comes with the opportunity to become like him. To have all that He has. To create like He does.

Write down your feelings about creation and creators:
_____
_____
_____
_____

Enid

It seems that our creator is absent from our lives. But not so. He continues to lend us breath. He continues to be mindful of us. He knows us. He is our creator.

Pause. Get quiet. Close your eyes. Ask, "Are you there?" Then wait with an open mind and heart. Just wait.

Write below what happened.

There will always be a connection between you and your creator. He has invested in you. He anticipates and celebrates your success. He is your greatest cheerleader. Trust that He has your best interests at heart. Past, present and future.

He loves you more than you can comprehend. Like a potter He took raw clay and molded it and fired it. Along the way His creation gets chipped, cracked, and broken. Sometimes misused. Sometimes forgotten. But He is never far away. He provides the glue, the helpers, the skills needed to recover and repair His creation.

Every step of the way He is mindful of your right to choose. He is patient and leaves it up to you whether you want to be repaired or restored. He waits patiently with love. When you are ready, He is there with all the necessary resources for you to heal and move forward. He patiently waits. He loves you. He is the potter and you are the clay.

Daniel

FOR YOU: A Guide to the Universe

NOTES

CHAPTER 3

The Plan of Happiness

There is a plan for you. A magnificent plan. One you played a part in. It began with the end in mind, all under the direction of a loving Father. The Father of us all.

We start with the beginning of your journey here to earth in the premortal existence. In this place your spirit dwelt with other spirits and with the Creator. You were taught and you developed relationships with other spirits. A council was held about the next step in the plan and two options were presented. One involved a Savior and the other a Dictator.

The first option allowed for your agency or choice. The second option took away your ability to choose. One third of the spirits in this place chose the second option. Those that chose this option would not receive a physical body. Their progression was stopped.

You were among those that chose to come to this earth and receive a body. Because of this choice other choices opened up for you. Your spirit with a body could now do things your spirit couldn't do as just a spirit. You shouted for joy at the opportunity you would have on earth. Preparations were made for you to have the gifts, talents, and tools you would need to be successful during your time on earth. Successful in your return to the Creator and to those you love. You did not come here to earth unprepared. So, why would you forget all of that and come with a clean slate?

It was all about the ability to choose and the love the Creator has for you. The plan allows for there to be good and bad. Joy and sorrow. Happiness and sadness. Because without one we wouldn't know the other. Our choices and the choices of others would make all the difference.

Through your experiences here on earth you would feel inklings of remembering things that felt right, normal and familiar to you. Your veil of forgetfulness was getting thinner in spots. Other people would come and go during your journey here. They would be your teachers, your mentors, and you theirs. Opportunities would present themselves for you to remember who you are and why you came, your purpose, your strengths and your family.

When you have completed what you were sent here to do, you will die and return to the world of spirits. In that world of spirits there is a paradise and a prison. Depending on your choices you will be sent to one or the other to await the judgment day.

While you wait, there will be teachers who will teach those willing to listen about the truths that will help them do what they need to do to return to live eternally with the Creator and their loved ones.

Each person that has ever lived on the earth will have earned their next step. For some the next step is a place to dwell with no more progression, and to others their choices on earth merited even more options and progression.

The Plan of Happiness

This is a plan. A plan of happiness. A plan where your choices determine your progression. A plan of empowerment and joy, of family and loved ones.

Walter

I always knew I had been alive somewhere before I was alive here on earth. I used to have dreams about a beautiful place where there was love, happiness, family, learning, growing, preparation, and knowledge. I always felt so safe and free and loved when I found myself in this place. I started writing down my experiences there. There is an order to all things in this place.

I recall a time when a few of us were directed to a square outdoors. We were seated on benches and were instructed to wait; someone would be coming to talk to us. As we waited, we visited with each other and wondered who was coming. We could feel His approach before we could see Him. No words were spoken as He entered the square where we were gathered. He stood at the edge of the square and gazed on each one of us.

The power He held was palpable, tangible, and we all felt it. There seemed to be a current of fire that surrounded Him, especially around His head and face. He had all our attention. As he began to speak, I knew why each one of us had been gathered there. He had an assignment for us, together and individually. It seemed as if His words were being written on my heart, never to be forgotten or misunderstood. We were to find each other and deliver the message He would give us. We would need certain gifts to be able to deliver the message and those gifts would be bestowed on us individually when He finished speaking with us.

As I looked around it seemed as if the faces of those there were also imprinted on my heart. I knew when I saw them on earth we would know each other, and we would remember. So far five of us have found each other; we have a few more to find.

At the conclusion of His instruction, each one of us came forward, one at a time, and He laid His hands on our heads and we were given the gifts we would need to deliver the message. The courage and confidence that were instilled in me made me feel that nothing could stop me from being able to deliver the message. As I listened to the other spirits receive their gifts, they were similar to mine but unique to each one of us.

As He departed it seemed as if the light got dimmer in the square where we were gathered. We all sat pondering for a time about what had just happened.

This is one of many experiences I have recorded about this beautiful place, for which I am amazed and grateful.

Sam

Who needs a plan? Life is meant to be lived and enjoyed as it comes. I didn't need a plan until one day life came crashing down around me. I was a very successful businessman. Had the world by the tail. I had the house, the car, the vacations, the clients and all the money I had ever dreamed of.

One evening on my way home from work I lost control of my car and went off an embankment. They tell me someone saw the accident and called for emergency crews. I was transported to a medical facility. Three months later I woke up to find my car was in a junkyard, my house had been vandalized, and my business had been taken over by someone else. My bank account had been drained by my medical bills.

Despite my family and friends, I didn't know how I would be able to pick up the pieces that were left of my life and go on. Day after day I thought of what to do next. I still had many weeks of rehabilitation ahead of me. I had a lot of time to think.

During a conversation with someone who was also recovering from an accident I asked him what he had to be so positive about. He usually had a smile on his face no matter what they were making him do. He told me that his accident and injuries were but a small moment in the big picture.

I had to ask, "What big picture?"

He told me God had a plan. A plan that started before we ever got to earth and one that would continue after we leave here. "And this brings you happiness?" I questioned.

He said, "Yes a deep happiness. I still get sad and experience sorrow, but deep in my soul I know this will pass."

I don't remember ever feeling the deep happiness he had described to me.

As the days and weeks stretched into months, we talked a little each time we saw each other. I usually asked questions and he answered them the best he could. I felt hope come back into my soul as my body healed. I felt like I was missing something very important in my life before the accident. But I didn't know that I could have a happiness like he did.

One night as I lay in bed, I saw myself healthy and strong with a wife and two children. We were happy and I knew it was the deep happiness my friend had talked about. I was overwhelmed with joy and gratitude. "How?" I wondered out loud. That moment seemed to be the life I was always meant to have.

So, I worked harder to recover physically. I opened a dialogue with God. I hoped He heard me. Five years have passed and that moment from that night so long ago is now reality.

Keep reading and you will find out how it came about.

Simpson

There was a time when I believed there was no God. But through a series of events I came to know otherwise. The first thing that happened was my niece died. She was two years old. We all missed her so much. I was angry that she was taken from us, especially as I saw the family distraught over her loss. It didn't make sense. Then my grandmother passed away. She was very old and had lived a good life. Then my husband fell and broke his neck, but recovered completely. He should have died, but he didn't.

My daughter had a baby boy in the middle of all this. He was born early and needed a lot of care. He stopped breathing a few times but today is healthy and happy.

I knew about the cycle of life and death but hadn't really thought about this cycle being part of a plan. Things started to make sense one day when I saw the words, "Heavenly Father has a plan for me." Who was this person who takes and gives randomly it seems? I have always wanted to believe there was an order to things. Randomness, when it comes to people's lives, has always seemed wrong to me.

So, I wondered who this Heavenly Father was and what His plan was. One night I had the most vivid dream. I was in a place

The Plan of Happiness

with my parents and grandparents. My children and grandchildren were there too. Everyone was there and we were playing and talking, and it was a beautiful place. I didn't recognize it. Everyone was healthy and happy. Then I realized we were all adults. I recognized everyone anyway.

Initially I was confused. Some I recognized from pictures. My parents came toward me and after some robust hugs and kisses I asked, "What is this place? Am I dead?" They laughed and said, "No, we haven't received our bodies yet. You are in heaven. The place we lived before we came to earth. We are all together in families. We support each other and learn about things together as we prepare to begin our journey on earth." They all seemed to have assignments of some sort and would come and go as their responsibilities dictated.

But what about me?

A beautiful being approached me and beckoned me to follow her. Eventually we arrived at a room that felt familiar. To me. I felt comfortable there. All around the room were things that symbolized the skills I was good at the things I was interested in, my job, my work and my family.

Our next step was a room where many people were gathered. One at a time spirits would make their way to the front of the room. Some words were exchanged, and the spirit sat in the only chair on the platform. Hands were placed on the spirit's head; heads were bowed and words were said. Then the spirit was escorted off the platform and out of the room.

I was so curious. Who are these people and those men and what are they doing? Why do I need to be here? My thoughts and questions came to a screeching halt when I noticed the next spirit making her way to the front of the room was me. I looked at my guide and she gave me a little wink letting me know that what I was seeing was really happening.

This time I could hear what was being said. They called me by name and asked if I was ready to receive my earthly assignment? "Yes," was all I could get out and I was escorted to the chair. Their hands felt warm on my head and then they spoke the most beautiful words about the talents and skills I would have. There were names that were mentioned of people I should find and that we would help each other accomplish the plan Heavenly Father had for us. Character traits were also mentioned that I would need to develop.

Some other words of encouragement were spoken and then when they were finished, I was escorted out of the room. My face was beaming with excitement and anticipation as I made my way out of the room. But I wanted to know who this Heavenly Father person is that has this plan for me that I seemed so excited about. She smiled and again I followed her.

The light around us seemed to be getting brighter and brighter until she stopped. The room we were in was beautiful, full of light. I saw a man approaching. I not only saw but felt him coming closer. I heard the words, "This is your Heavenly Father." He wrapped his arms around me and hugged me and whispered my name. I felt wrapped in a love I can't describe. He led me to some chairs that faced each other and said, "Let's talk. I understand you have many questions."

When I woke up, I laid very still. All that had happened in the dream was still so vivid and real. But was it? I got up and wrote down all I could remember. From that day forward my life was never the same. I had a purpose. I understood what it was. I knew what and who I was searching for. He knew what had changed in

The Plan of Happiness

me. I worked on the skills and talents I had been offered. I knew I was loved and had a purpose in His plan.

Sandy

I am from a faraway land. My story is for you. I want you to know why you came here.

I came to this land as a small child. My family believed there was a bigger purpose than being born, living and dying on this earth. They talked about it often. We made up stories about what we would be doing in heaven when we were all together again. It was a fun game to play.

Eventually both my parents passed on from this earth life and it wasn't until I was on my deathbed that I remembered that game we played. My mind went to so many questions. Would they be waiting for me? Would we truly be together again or was it just an empty fantasy? When I passed from this earth life, I was greeted by not only my mother and father but by my grandparents, aunts, uncles, cousins, and others. The game we had played so long ago was real! Other families had very few members that were together in one place. I understood those that were missed had either never made covenants on earth or hadn't been true to the covenants they had made. At first, I had a lot of questions and there was much discussion. I found out that the people weren't so much missing as they were in a place where they could learn and have an opportunity to make better choices or not. The reunions I witnessed when those family members were reunited were precious. I have since become a teacher to help those who have been separated from their families because of the choices they made on earth.

I am one of many teachers who teach the truths that will help them make better choices so ultimately, they can be with their families again and enjoy all that is possible for each one of us through eternity.

Gerald

Sometimes I looked at the stars and wondered why I was here now and what was next. My grandmother would tell us stories whenever she could get us to listen.

One of my favorite stories was the one she told us of a family that lived a very long time ago. The dad happened to be an important man and there were lots of kids. Each one of the kids had an assignment. Some got land, some got wealth, and some were given works to do. Their great grandfather was also a very important man and God promised him that he would have so much posterity that there would be too many to count.

He was also promised that if he kept his promises to God then he would have everything God had, including his power. His family could too. One of the sons had two sons. One of those sons was tasked with gathering all who would listen and teaching them the truths that would make them the most happy. These truths would make it possible for families to be together after they die and forever and ever.

First, I wanted the power that God had, that sounded amazing. Of course, I wanted to be with my family always. When I asked my grandmother how all this was supposed to happen, she

The Plan of Happiness

said that was a story for another time. I never got to hear that story because she passed away soon after she told me that.

One day, as my mother was sorting through my grandmother's things, she found a note. It said, "Read this to Oscar when he asks how to get the power of God and how to be with us always." She brought me the note. I was a grown man by this time. I had looked up at the stars so many times always wondering why I was here on the earth now and what happens after this earth life.

With the note was a piece of paper that said, "Find me." "Find who?" I asked my mother. She didn't know either. I went to where my grandmother's body was entombed and asked out loud, "Is this what you mean?" No answer. I couldn't figure out what "find me" meant, and life went on.

I had heard of a man that performed miracles and was somewhat curious about how he did such amazing things. I visited my grandmother's grave often and talked about many things with her. But there was never a response.

About this time, I started hearing people talk of this miracle worker and how angry they were because of what he was doing. The next thing I heard was that he had been executed. Some were upset and very sad. Others were satisfied that justice had been done. A few days later, I was visiting my grandmother like I always did. I was reflecting on the note she left, the one that said, "Find me," when I felt her presence growing stronger and stronger. Confused I stood up and I watched as her body materialized before my eyes and became animated. Her eyes met mine. I was transfixed. I had no idea what I had just witnessed. She came towards me with outstretched arms and such a beautiful smile. As we embraced, she whispered, "You found me my precious boy, you found me."

We sat and talked for what seemed like hours. She explained to me about the man who did all the miracles, the same one that was executed. Because of what he did some of the graves were opened and they were resurrected. Their spirits and bodies reunited, never to be separated again.

She stayed for a while. She was warm and drank from my water flask. I sat for some time pondering on what had just transpired. She told me many more things. I had many questions. When I finally went home, I had some amazing stories to tell.

Oscar

My story begins in a faraway place. Some call it the premortal existence and others call it the life before life. I, along with everyone else, was taught about where we were, the earth that was being prepared for us, and what would happen after our earth life based on our choices.

I had begun to worry. What if I screwed up? What if I went to earth and didn't make the choices I wanted to make so I could have the outcome I wanted? I worried about this for some period of time and finally I asked one of my teachers what to do.

They told me to figure out exactly what I wanted the outcome to be and to arrange things so that clues would be left for me all along my earthly journey to keep me on the path to the outcome I wanted. "Okay," I said. "How do I do that?"

The Plan of Happiness

They sent me to an expert in how to arrange for the clues. I was almost giddy when I arrived at this office. I was asked what outcome I wanted, and we discussed and planned and discussed some more. Finally, we had identified all the clues I would need and when and where they would present themselves.

This all came with a warning. I wouldn't remember any of this planning and the discussion or my life before earth. I knew that, but I didn't really understand it until I heard it in the warning.

There was more worry and fear until one day a beloved friend of mine sat me down, looked into my eyes and said, "We will help each other remember and there are others that will help too." I felt better.

Fast forward to today. I found the clues. I found those that helped me. I even remembered many things about the life before earth. The outcome I prepared and planned for is within my reach.

Look for your clues. If you don't think you have found any, keep looking or look around with different eyes. They are there and waiting to be found or waiting to be acknowledged. Good hunting.

What clues have you found on your journey so far?

_____
_____
_____
_____

Who have you found that has helped you?

_____
_____

FOR YOU: A Guide to the Universe

_____
_____

Mathew

★ ✹ ★

When was the last time you experienced joy? Did you know that is one of the reasons you are here on earth? If you haven't felt joy ever, or in a very long time, do you know why?

_____
_____
_____
_____

Define what joy is to you.

_____
_____
_____
_____

Joy comes with sorrow. That's just how things are. If you haven't made a list of what brings you joy, write down below all things that bring you joy or could bring you joy.

_____
_____
_____
_____

The Plan of Happiness

Pick three of the items on your list and write down what you can do to experience those things more often. Remember that joy is one of the reasons you are here on the earth.

_____

_____

_____

_____

Cherry

★ ★ ★

"Life is hard and then you die," was what I was always told. I hated to hear that because my life was hard and then I died. Imagine my surprise when I found out that death doesn't mean gone.

Then the learning, instruction, discussing, questions and "aha"s began. Wow were my mind and eyes and heart opened. Opportunities were presented to me and I took the good ones. I learned why my life was hard. I learned about life and death and what came before and what was next. Most importantly, love made the hard easier. Hang in there. Good stuff is ahead for you if you want it. It can also be part of your now. You don't have to die like me to figure this out. Find and embrace what will make your "hard" easier and embrace it wholeheartedly. Let it change your life for the better.

What is your "hard"?

_____

_____

___

What would make your "hard" a little easier?

___

Charles

When I was a young lad my dad would tell me stories. To me he was the greatest storyteller known to man. He occasionally would tell this story:

There were three trolls who lived a very long time ago. They were siblings and most days they got along. They lived in the trees. Each troll had their own house in the trees. The houses weren't very big, but they were comfortable and cozy.

The troll who lived in the treehouse closest to the ground was on the grumpy side. His name was Montel. He never went up to the other two treehouses to visit his brothers, but they would come down to see him. They would hunt for food together and swim in the lakes. Sometimes a troll or two would come into their part of the woods. Montel would require payment from those who passed by and would heckle them as they moved on. His treehouse was cluttered, dirty and run down. There was trash all around because he didn't care.

The Plan of Happiness

Terry was the troll whose treehouse was a wee bit higher than Montel's. He didn't mind when other trolls passed through their part of the forest and he never required any money from them. He took pride in his treehouse and kept it clean and tidy. It was hard to visit his brother below him because he preferred not to be around him when he was grumpy, which was often. Sometimes Montel's grumpiness rubbed off on Terry and Terry became grumpy himself.

Purcel was the troll that lived in the highest treehouse. He loved being the highest because he could see all the forest when he climbed up on the roof. There were flowers in the window boxes that hung at the base of all the windows. His treehouse was the nicest of all three because he kept it in pristine condition from top to bottom. The surfaces gleamed. Everyone in the forest liked Purcel and he liked them. He was kind to everyone and helped when anything heavy needed to be moved, demolished or carried somewhere else.

Purcel always visited his two brothers even though they never came to see him. He was always bringing their favorite troll soup or freshly picked mushrooms to share with them. He loved to sit with them in front of their tree houses and visit while they ate or snacked.

At this point in the story my dad would ask all of us if we had had a Montel, Terry or Purcel day. We would think for a few minutes and if we picked Montel, he knew we had been grouchy or mean or had made some choices that we weren't proud of. If we had a Terry day, he knew we were making better choices than a Montel day, but there had been a few things that we could improve on.

He was pleased when we had had a Purcel day. No matter what our day was like we knew he loved us no matter what. He would encourage us to be the troll in the highest treehouse and we always tried to do our best.

When we were older, he told us that we would be rewarded in the next life depending on which "troll lifestyle" we had chosen to live while on the earth.

We all wanted to be like Purcel because we knew our dad would be rewarded the highest treehouse. I think he knew something we didn't and tried to teach through the stories he told. We now tell them to our children, and they all love trolls.

What did you learn from this story?

_____

_____

_____

_____

Smedley

I spent a lot of time meditating. I was an avid reader and read everything I could get my hands on. The books about near death experiences really made me curious. I wanted to know what to expect once I made the crossover from life on earth to death and who knows where.

My curiosity got the best of me and one day during my meditation I found myself in a glorious place. As I approached the person nearest me, I asked where we were. They told me we were

The Plan of Happiness

in the spirit world; the place we go after we die. For a moment I was in shock and then I realized this is what I had wanted to know for myself for so long.

I wanted to see everything and so I began to walk. I was greeted with smiles everywhere I went. This was a happy place. Eventually I came to a place where the people inside looked anxious. Some looked sad and some looked mad.

I asked someone close by why these people looked like they did. They explained that these people had made choices during their earth lives that kept them in the dark. The people on this side had made choices that enabled them to live in the light.

Can the people get out of that place and into this place? "Yes," I was told, "But they have to be taught and accept truth and, with help from people still on earth, they can come out of the darkness and into the light."

I thanked them for the information and, as I was pondering about what they had told me, I found myself back in the room I was meditating in. There I sat unsure about what had just happened. I wrote down the experience so I wouldn't forget and so began my quest to be one of the people that lives in the light when I passed from this life to the next.

Barry

Before we came to earth two plans were presented to all who would inhabit this earth. The first plan involved honoring the ability to choose and receiving a physical body. The second plan took away individual choice and put it solely in the control of one person. You and I were there. Many of those we loved were seduced by the presenter of the second plan. A vote was taken. Two-thirds wanted the plan with the ability to choose. The other third decided to relinquish their ability to choose and not have a physical body.

The war that ensued after the votes were taken was heartbreaking. It continues to rage. Those who chose the second plan want to influence and corrupt the other two-thirds. They continue to try and influence those with physical bodies while they live on the earth. They are angry. They live in darkness. They want us to be miserable like they are. Those with the ability to choose, whether they have yet to come to earth or have already come and gone, can influence those living on the earth as well.

So the battle will continue until the light is greater than the darkness.

Carlos

Do you have a plan? "A plan for what?" you might ask. Would it surprise you to know that you are right now participating in a plan? A plan of happiness. What part are you playing? Or would you play your part better if you knew what this plan of happiness was?

I am guessing your answer was, "Yes." But you might be a little upset that you are part of a plan you knew nothing about. On the other hand, you might be excited to discover there is a grand plan that was orchestrated for you to be as happy as you possibly can for a very long time, eternity to be exact. It goes like this:

- Live in a spirit world
- Come to the mortal world

The Plan of Happiness

- Make mistakes
- Be provided with a Savior, Redeemer
- Leave the mortal world
- Live in a spirit world until the time of accountability
- Be accountable for choices made in the mortal and spirit worlds
- Be rewarded with the life you chose by your actions and thoughts.

There are and have been choices all along the way. You are the one who determines the level of happiness you want and are willing to live for.

What will you choose?

_____

_____

_____

_____

Jerry

★ ✹ ★

Those were the days when I didn't care what the consequences of my actions were. I didn't care whether I lived or died. I didn't about another soul. Until I looked around and all my friends were either married, with someone, had a few kids, good jobs, finished school, starting their career and they seemed to be generally happy and living for something I didn't know anything about.

When I looked at me, I had none of what they had and realized I wanted the direction, the stability, and the connection they had to others. They had been kind to me, but in the process of stepping back and looking, I realized they had to disconnect from me in a way so they could move forward. I was separated from the real connections that had meant everything to me.

What happened to me? Why had I made such different choices? I thought I was happy, but I wasn't. I was searching for what they had: direction, meaning, and connection.

What are you connected to?

_____
_____
_____
_____

What type of connection is important to you?

_____
_____
_____
_____

What are you going to do to establish and nurture the connections you want?

_____
_____
_____
_____

Courtney

The Plan of Happiness

I met a man who changed my life. He was a humble man. Many hated him for the things he did. He lived in my hometown. He grew up with us, but then he went away.

Years later I heard stories about a man who was stirring up trouble. When someone told me he was close by, I went to see. As I got closer, I recognized him. I backed away so he wouldn't see me, so I could observe what it was he was doing that was making everyone so upset.

He was sitting on a stool. He was answering questions and listening to the people that surrounded him. Most of them were peacefully listening. Some of them were standing off from the group with arms folded and with serious looks on their faces. He was aware of all of them and made eye contact with them occasionally.

The people began dispersing to go their separate ways and I felt it was time for me to approach him. He saw me coming and the expression on his face went from looking at me to recognizing me. We embraced and we walked. We talked of what had happened since we had left home. I told him I was surprised it was him whom all the uproar was about. He seemed the same but different somehow.

Whenever he was near to my home he would come with some friends and spend some time with me and my family. As time went on, I came to know what had changed him. He was no longer here for himself; he was here for you and me and for all of us.

The day he was crucified was one of great sadness and sorrow. When I heard he was alive again my gratitude and understanding was beyond expression. He knew me. He loved me. He died for me. He lives for me.

And you.

Cecily

There was a time when the world was not so much in commotion. Times were simpler. Life was not so complicated. It was then I came to know the Savior. My husband was a simple fisherman. He was a very good fisherman. We lived where everyone had something to do with fishing. We were good people. One day my husband came through the door at his usual time. Tired after a day of work. Quiet. He came to me and held me for the longest time. No words were said, but I sensed sadness and love all mixed together.

We sat down and he explained to me what had happened.

A man came to where they were and said he would make them "fishers of men." He said if he went with this man he wouldn't be fishing, and he would not be home very much. He didn't want to leave me and our family, but somehow, he knew we would be okay. We would have what we needed. He would miss us every minute.

As he talked my heart burned within me. Tears filled our eyes. He knew he had my love, my support, and my prayers. In the morning he was gone.

Weeks, months, and years went by. We did have what we needed. We were never without. He and the other "fishers of men" stopped in when they could. Each time he came home, even for a few hours, I could see the change in him.

The Plan of Happiness

Then things got a little scary. He and the other men and their families were in danger. The Savior Jesus Christ was killed. The men were sent to tell his story and to share why He came and why He died and where He was now.

Eventually, I learned of my husband's death. But I knew I would see him again and we would never again be separated. I wasn't the only one whose husband left his nets and family to ensure we could always be together.

Chare

Do you feel like a small speck of nothing in this huge expanse of space? When you look up at the stars do you feel insignificant? When you lose your job do you feel like a loser? When someone criticizes you, do you feel like there is something wrong with you? When you see someone with the body, the muscles, the hair, the teeth, the clothes, the job, the family you wish you had, do you shrink a little each time that happens?

What if I told you that you are significant, you are more than this life itself? What if I told you that if you weren't breathing the universe would fold in on itself?

You aren't just part of the plan; you ARE the plan!

Let that sink in for a bit. What was your first reaction?

_____
_____
_____
_____

Can you feel it? The part of you that is waking up. The part that hears the words and knows, and feels their truth? You might need to get out of your own way so you can connect to these truths!

_____

_____

_____

_____

Standing

I am in this book because my story is important. Not more important than the other but it needs telling. My family immigrated to a country that was very foreign to us. I was a small child at the time and unaware of the difficulties of making such a move. We were trading our difficult situation for another. There were four of us: my father, mother, sister and me.

Instead of things getting better, they got worse and then war broke out. My father was being hunted. He had to go into hiding as soon as the war started. People were watching the place where we lived. We didn't dare leave the house. We didn't know what would happen. Eventually someone my mother knew and trusted helped us leave. It was a long time before we stopped. Finally, my mother seemed to relax. We were safe.

One day alarms sounded in the village we were living in. My mother wasn't sure what to do but we fled to the mountains. There were many other people fleeing too. Everyone was scared. My sister and I were terrified and trying so hard not to cry. I

The Plan of Happiness

remember a loud sound and then everything was quiet. I was still holding my sister's hand and could see our mother ahead of us. I recognized many people from the village.

We were all dead. My mother turned around and threw her arms around us. I could feel her shaking. Someone touched her on her shoulder and as she let us go and turned, I saw a man who seemed to be glowing. He held my mother and then knelt down in front of my sister and me. His eyes were filled with tears, but we knew immediately he was safe, we were safe, and everything would be okay. Time felt different in this place. We didn't eat or sleep. Everything was beautiful. My sister and I made friends with a bunch of other kids.

I want you to know about this place and that man. His name is Jesus and He loves me, and He loves you. Don't be afraid. Everything will be okay.

Simpson

NOTES

CHAPTER 4

Your Place in the Plan

I was present when the assignments were made as to which dispensations of time each group of spirits would be sent to. Within each group there were assignments made. Some would be leaders, and some would be followers, but all had the capacity and the opportunity to progress according to the plan.

After these assignments were made, individual assignments were made, and all spirits went to work learning and preparing to come to earth at their appointed time. We were assigned this last dispensation. The one that would welcome our brother and Savior Jesus Christ for the second time. Because we were assigned to come during this last dispensation, we have had an immense amount of time to prepare, to learn, to watch, to assist others, and to be ready. Ready to come and fulfill our assignments.

You have a unique purpose and assignment that only you can complete. It is up to you to discover what that assignment is and to choose to fulfill it or not. No one else can do what you came here to do. You are that important.

Leslie

I feel like shouting for joy every day because I am here on the earth at this time. Of all the dispensations of time to come to earth I would have picked this one to come to, to be born and live during. I wasn't always like this. The world seems to be in chaos and there are bad things happening. I found myself afraid and depressed about life in general. Then I started to notice little moments of goodness and strength all around me in people, families, communities, and nations. Eventually my fears dissolved, and my depression turned into anticipation of the next moment of goodness, courage and strength I would witness or be part of. Now I get up each day looking forward to what I will witness and experience.

Patsy

There was a time when I questioned my existence. What good was I, or anyone around me? My life meant nothing to anyone, and I had nothing to offer anyone anyway.

It was the strangest thing. One day as I was walking to my car, I noticed a pamphlet on the ground. It had been driven over a few times and looked a little ragged. I picked it up to throw it away and a word caught my eye. Purpose. The word was purpose. Looking closer I could see it was part of a phrase. It read, "You have a purpose." I stared at these words and time seemed to stand still. Did I? Did I truly have a purpose beyond surviving? I felt myself wanting to believe that my life meant something.

It was in that moment something seemed to spark to life in my soul. I did have a purpose. Somehow, I knew this deep, deep down inside of my core. But what was it?

My phone rang and the distraction from my thoughts lasted until I got home and found the tattered pamphlet in my bag. I must have put it in there without thinking when my phone rang. I slumped down on the sofa and a tear puddled in my eye. Oh, how I wanted to believe I had a purpose.

So I asked the universe, "Is there a reason I am here in this moment in time?"

The words I heard changed my life! "You have a work to do that only you can do. I and others are here to support you in accomplishing this work. Don't be afraid. Only believe."

For a moment I barely breathed. Had I really heard what I just heard? Was it all in my head? I found some paper and wrote down the words exactly as I heard them. Every chance I got I looked at those words. I carried the paper they were written on wherever I went. Life seemed to have found me again, maybe for the first time. In the most unexpected places, I found or became aware of, clues as to this work I and only I could do. Eventually I knew what my work on this earth, at this time, was to be. AND I DID IT.

Sandra

I was there with you when we shouted for joy at the choice, we made to have a Savior and receive a body on earth so we could continue to progress. After the council meeting was over, we all went our separate ways. I was scheduled to go to earth in the early

1900s. My assignment in heaven was to teach those who were preparing to go to earth. You might wonder how I could prepare others to go where I hadn't been yet, but I assure you I knew what I was talking about. I was allowed to go to earth in my spirit form and observe people living there. Once my training was over, I was one of many earth instructors to help prepare those who would soon be born on earth. My specialty was to teach them about how they would be using their bodies.

How, as a spirit, they would be joined to a physical body and be able to do things they had only dreamt about in heaven.

At first, they would be a bit disoriented. They would not be able to speak or control their bodies. They would also start forgetting about heaven. That was very upsetting to some of my students. So we talked about how at first we wouldn't remember, but as we grew and increased in knowledge and gained life experience we would get glimpses of truths and start remembering. That encouraged them a bit.

I had to warn them that other spirits, who would never have bodies, would want to use their bodies. They needed to be strong and not let the spirits have access to their bodies. This was also upsetting to my students and they didn't think I was very fair. Then we would talk about agency and our ability to choose, just like those spirits had the ability to choose as well.

But with our physical bodies we had a great advantage over those that didn't. We can do things they never could.

When it was my turn to go to earth and receive my body, I was so excited. It wasn't until I was 41 years old that I remembered that I was a teacher in heaven before I was born. I found it very interesting that I ended up becoming a teacher here on earth. And yep, you guessed it, I was a teacher of how to keep physical bodies healthy and strong so my students could fulfill their purpose on the earth.

What did you do in heaven before you came to earth?

_____

_____

_____

_____

Cherrie

Sometimes I question my purpose. It is during these times that my world seems to fall apart. It starts with, "What's the use? Nothing I do matters. No one cares whether I live or die. If I was gone tomorrow, no one would notice."

Hopelessness wiggles its way in and soon I withdraw and disengage from everything good around me. Without fail, something happens, or someone shows up and wakes me out of my state of lostness and puts me back on track to remember my purpose and my why.

Let me illustrate. My cousins and I are close. We grew up in the same town together and spent as much time as we could together. We all eventually went our separate ways except for me and my cousin Luke. We went into business together and were making good money. The business was doing great. The economy shifted and what I specialized in shifted into something I had no clue how to do. In our discussions about what to do we talked about multiple options. The best one for me left me with plenty of money and no job. I could feel things starting to fall apart as I panicked about whether I had a purpose or not. Was my purpose the job I had? The money didn't interest me if I had no purpose beyond it. Weeks and then months went by. I didn't leave my house. Hygiene was not something that occurred to me on a daily basis. My friends and family were tired of trying to help. I didn't know what to do and I didn't care.

One night I was dreaming and saw myself in a beautiful place with happy people all around me. They all seemed to have something to do. They were all doing different things. As I walked among them, I was drawn to a building. I went inside and there was one chair in the middle of the room and a movie was playing on a screen. I sat down in the chair and realized it was me and my life. As I watched I could see how happy I was before I left the business but could tell that something was missing. I watched the part about me leaving the business and then how my life deteriorated. "Was it that bad?" I wondered. But the movie kept going and I saw a dressed, clean shaven, bathed man, who looked happy. I was confused about what had happened.

I saw myself working at a new business, one I had created. I saw the happiness and gratitude I went through life with. At night, before I got into bed, I saw myself praying and telling God how grateful I was for my life, my family, for Him and for my reason for being on the earth at this time. That's where my dream ended. I woke up with a face full of hair, surrounded by old food wrappers, dirty clothes, beverage containers, and the smell of someone who hadn't bathed in I forget how many days.

The shock of my life I had seen on the movie screen in the future and what I saw right in front of me propelled me up and out of bed and into the shower. Then with all the facial hair gone

Your Place in the Plan

I cleaned my house from top to bottom. I sat on my sofa that I hadn't seen the cushions of for weeks because of all the litter and began my search for that purpose I was so grateful for in the movie.

I HAD A PURPOSE!

Joseph

Certain aspects of life on earth have bothered me for a very long time. At the top of the list is: "Why me? Why here? Why now?" I look around and don't see the answers to any of those questions. I had asked these three questions of many people in many different contexts and never got an acceptable answer until this one day. I was having a particularly bad day and grumbling about something under my breath that my friend overheard. She asked what was wrong and I told her for the thousandth time that the "whys" were bothering me again. It is as if I were blowing in the wind with no flagpole, kite string, or attachments.

She commented that that seemed a bit dramatic. I told her, "Well that's how it feels, fluttering, trembling, getting a little tattered and wearing a little thin in places." She threw up her hands and walked out. She was no help and I continued with my grumbling.

In the mail was a letter from my mom. Something made me want to open the envelope now instead of how I usually waited to read her letters to me. As I opened it a sticker fell out that said:

"Why me? Why here? Why now?"

Because we need you.

Because they need you.

Because God needs you.

She said she found it at a gas station and thought about me because I am always looking for answers to my list of questions.

I couldn't believe it. It was my why. Who knew it was that simple? Happiness exploded all over my face. I could have squeezed her.

Let the pondering and meditation begin.

Because we need you.

Because they need you.

Because God needs you.

What do those statements mean to you?

_____

_____

_____

_____

Sarah

Chances are I have never met you and never will. But I have something to say to you. I hope you will listen and feel my words.

You are here at this time for an important reason. No one that has been born, or ever will be, can do what you can do at this time in the history or future of the earth. I hear you scoffing and wondering why you ever picked this book up. Let me say it a little differently.

You are unique. You are one of a kind and God knows you better than you know yourself. There have been a lot of people come and go on the earth up to this point and it is not an accident you were saved to come now.

Keep reading. There's more.

Your parents are unique. Your family is unique. Which makes you even more unique.

Now I hear you saying, "So? Big deal. I am a nobody. So what if there's no one else like me?" And I say that means no one can do what you can do, or accomplish what you can accomplish, or be who you can be. The people around you need you. There are people you will touch because you have the skills, the personality, the understanding, the empathy, the words, the deeds, the desires, the life experiences, the family, the smile, the tears, the helping hands, the laugh … I could go on and on.

If you don't, who will?

What makes you unique?

_____
_____
_____
_____

Sidney

My greatest fear in life is that I will miss something important that has to do with my happiness. My life had been peaceful. Nothing exciting. Until one day I met a woman who seemed to be full of happiness and she was always doing for others. Her life was peaceful but directed outwards. My life was peaceful, but I was content to focus on myself.

She would include me sometimes, inviting me to go here or there to help someone individually, or others who were in need. Eventually, I started looking for an opportunity to give, or those opportunities seemed to find me.

My whole life seemed to shift. My heart expanded and my peace deepened in a way I had never imagined. I couldn't get enough. I made new friends and when I needed help, I was surrounded by those I had helped. Some of them who had never met me, but became aware of me, came when they were needed most.

My peace comes from focusing outwards in ways I can help someone else.

Who needs you right now? Today?

_____

_____

_____

_____

Solange

If I could shout from the rooftops. If I could look into your eyes. If I could touch your soul to make you hear me. I would say:

You are needed!

You are important!

You are unique!

Your Place in the Plan

You are special!
You are loved!
No really! You came for this time, this place, and these people. Now find out why!

Sophronia

I was feeling sorry for myself and aimlessly going through life. Sometimes wondering what difference would it make if I had never come to this earth? I had a good job. Good family. Not perfect, but it was the same old thing.

One night I was startled awake and I was frantic. I reached for my wife and scared her. I held her as I sobbed for the longest time. Then it occurred to me it was only a dream and my heart started to slow. I could breathe easier. Then I told her what had happened.

Apparently, I had dreamed of a life I wasn't in. My precious children had never been born. My wife had married someone else. In the dream I searched and searched to find evidence that I was somewhere. I went to the neighbor we had helped when their basement flooded. They didn't even live there. I went to my place of work and someone else was at my desk. I went to my parents and they were dead. Finally, exhausted, I sat down on the side of the road and with my head in my hands I sobbed and sobbed.

That is when I woke up.

My wife was real. My children were alive. My job was there for me when I arrived the next morning. I mattered. This life is the life I created.

I can do better. I can love more. I can see where my presence changed things. I can be grateful for every minute of every day.

It does matter that I am here, now, in this place with these people.

Smithy

Such were the days of plenty. When there was more than enough to go around. We were feeling pretty good about ourselves. It was easy to share when there was so much bounty. Gradually as the seasons came and went there was less bounty and more mouths to feed. Some people hoarded while others went without. Tempers rose and patience departed. We dreamt of the past and wondered why. Why did we have to suffer? Why was there so much greed and so much less sharing? One of us returned after having been gone for years. He was appalled at how so many had become so selfish and withdrawn when they remembered them as good and happy people.

He called all the villagers to a meeting and we waited until all were present. There was murmuring and complaining. No one seemed happy to be there. We all wondered why. Then he told all of us how disappointed he was. He remembered how the villagers were always helping each other and sharing what they had. How happy we were. He wanted us to remember. He waited. He had seen the world outside our village and had clung to the life he remembered in our village.

"It is not an accident that this has happened to you. It is easy to be happy and inclusive when there is more, and to spare. The true test comes when there isn't enough and there are those in need. You are here now in this time and in this place to pull from deep inside you, who you truly are."

The expressions on some of the villagers seemed to lighten up as they looked around at their friends and family and remembered. Villagers that hadn't spoken in years left the meeting chatting like old friends, because they were.

The whole village changed after that meeting. There was less bounty and more mouths to feed, but everyone knew it was up to them to remember and to help each other.

Hanover

Hearts are funny things. They beat, they break, they flutter, they murmur, they have holes in them, they stop, they hold feelings, they hurt, and sometimes they guide us.

Have you heard the saying, "You will know in your heart?" How is that possible?

All these stories and letters and writings are here in this book for your heart to respond to. Maybe you felt your heart swell a little or a lot. Maybe it felt like your heart was stopping because the feelings you were experiencing were almost overwhelming. Maybe your heart felt pinched because it was a truth you didn't want to hear or accept. Maybe your heart affected your eyes and tears came out.

Listen to your heart. Let it help you. Trust it.

What is your heart telling you right now?

_____

_____

FOR YOU: A Guide to the Universe

_____

_____

Huber

★ ✹ ★

In this chapter you have heard many different perspectives, from many kinds of people, in many different circumstances. Their messages were for you. It has been their wish to help you understand that there is a reason you are on the earth at this time, in this place, with these people. There is a plan and it is for you.

You and you alone make a difference in the world. There is something to do here that no one can do but you.

We encourage you to write down any thoughts, feelings, or ideas that are coming to you while you read or while you are pondering.

_____

_____

_____

_____

_____

_____

You have a story that will be told one day.

Jenny

★ ✹ ★

CHAPTER 5

The Laws and Truths We Function Within While We Sojourn on the Earth

We are all bound by laws, universal laws, that aren't the breakable kind. You may know about them, you may not. One of those laws has to do with your ability to choose. Some call it agency.

Wars have been fought over a people's right to choose and many have lost their lives to protect that right. You make choices everyday about simple and sometimes important things. You came to this earth with an inherent ability to know if the choices you are presented with are good or bad. Over time, that inherent ability can become skewed.

One part of this universal law is that even though you are free to make the choices you are not free to choose the consequences. To take away another's ability to choose is a serious act. This means a parent makes choices for his or her children until the children can make choices for themselves. You chose to come to earth, receive a body, and have the ability to make more choices. You learn from your choices, whether they are good or bad. The consequences give it away. In the beginning the consequences of your choices can be very dramatic and painful. So you learn not to do that again if you don't want that consequence. You may decide that you don't care about the consequences, but they come anyway.

No matter what your choices have been, to this point, you can choose to make better ones from here on out.

This is a universal law.

Amanda

Another universal law or truth is that there is life after death. (These universal laws have been debated from the beginning of time, but the debate has never been able to change the laws.) There will be a reckoning. You will be held accountable for your choices and your actions. There is no negotiating out of this.

Let me give you an example. On earth I made a choice that resulted in the death of a loved one. It was a choice I made on my own. As a result, once I passed out of this earthly existence, I found myself in a place where my choices were limited based on a universal law.

Eventually I was given opportunities to make choices that, with the help of others and a Redeemer, meant I was able to leave that place. I was afforded choices to help me progress to a much better place.

The Laws and Truths We Function Within

Because this earth life isn't the end of your progression, it gives you a different, broader perspective. This enables you to better see the bigger picture.

Harold

One very important truth that you often overlook or ignore is that you are responsible for your thoughts. You may argue that other people put thoughts in your head. This is true but what you do with those thoughts are your responsibility. Whether you reject the ideas that come with the thoughts, or entertain the ideas to the point they become part of who you are, is up to you.

An example would be when someone tells you that you are stupid. You are responsible for whether you reject the idea or incorporate it into who you are. You can complicate this whole process of thoughts and ideas, but simplifying the process looks something like this:

1. You hear a thought, good or bad.
2. You reject a thought because you know it is detrimental or incongruent with who you are.
3. You welcome the thought because you know it is true and it is congruent with who you truly are.
4. You let the thought or idea simmer in your mind as to whether you will reject it or welcome it. This may take some time. You will bounce the thought or idea off your belief systems, your life experiences, and the voices in your head.

Be careful what thoughts or ideas you entertain because they can become part of who you are. It is difficult to weed out the ones you don't want there, but it is possible to remove them.

You may call the voices in your head, your conscience, your intuition, your inspiration, the Devil, your mom, your dad, your granny. In the end you get to decide which of the voices you listen to. You get to decide which to keep and which to let go, which to believe and which to reject.

Don't be a victim of your thoughts. Choose wisely and live the life that brings you the most peace and happiness.

Tamra

You are either progressing or regressing. You are on a path, moving forward along it or backward. Every choice you make propels you further on the path or back to where you were before the choice was made. Some may say they are comfortable with where they are on the path but if there is no stretching or growth they are regressing.

At this moment, where do you see yourself on this path of life?

_____
_____
_____
_____

You might ask, "What difference does it make which direction I am going?"

You have unlimited potential. The knowledge you gain here on earth is the only thing you will take with you when you leave

The Laws and Truths We Function Within

this earthly existence. It is not a competition. With knowledge comes power to be used for good or bad.

Knowledge comes from books, education, life experience, testing and proving, failing and trying again. Wisdom is what you do with the knowledge you have. You are here to make choices and gain knowledge and return to those that love you. Let your heart help with your decision. Trust that you can know what you need to do, or not do, to move forward on this path of life; the path where failure is not an option as long as you try again.

Where do you see this path taking you?

_____

_____

_____

_____

If it is not the destination you are seeking what must you do to get back on the right path? The path whose destination is what you truly desire?

_____

_____

_____

_____

Paulo

There are other universal laws that haven't been mentioned. Some of them are the law of cause and effect, the law of perpetual transmutation, the law of like attracts like, and the law of creation. Each one of the laws, if you work within their parameters, help you progress, help you grow, and help you succeed at whatever you put our mind to.

God wants you to succeed that is why you are here. Is there one law or truth that spoke to you in this chapter?

_____
_____
_____
_____

Is there one that you want to learn more about?

_____
_____
_____
_____

A list of some of the universal laws and brief explanations of each are below.

Harriet

The Laws and Truths We Function Within

UNIVERSAL LAWS

The Law of Vibration
Everything has a vibration or frequency that responds to like vibrations or frequencies.

~

The Law of Cause and Effect or Karma
Whatever you put out in the world will return to you.

~

The Law of Polarity
Everything in the Universe has an opposite.

~

The Law of Vacuum
Whenever a space is created, nature fills it.

~

The Law of Gender and Gestation
Everything is made of female and male energy.

~

The Law of Rhythm
There are cycles, patterns, and flow.

~

The Law of Relativity
Everything just is. We put our own judgments on things and label them good or bad.

~

The Law of Perpetual Transmutation
Everything is constantly changing into and out of form.

~

The Law of Oneness
Everything in the Universe is connected to everything else.

~

The Law of Correspondence
Patterns repeat themselves. What you think and feel on the inside, you create on the outside.

~

The Law of Action
To manifest what you desire, you have to take actions that support your intentions.

CHAPTER 6

How to See and Recognize Truth and What Stops You from Seeing It

Most people think truth is related to their upbringing, their life experience, their values, their beliefs, their gender and so on. But truth is things as they really are, as they were, and as they will be.

So how do we know what things really are?

Let me give you a simple example. Because my aunt was mean and grouchy, I avoided her as much as I could. When I was older my mom told me my aunt wasn't always like that, but she had a disease that left her in constant pain. The truth was she was a kind and giving person.

I couldn't see the truth. I would have treated her differently had I known, or would I? I hope I would have treated her with kindness even though she scared me a little.

So how do we know what is truth? Do we need x-ray lenses? Do we need a magic ball? No, I think we need some compassion.

Mathew

My truth is different from your truth, or is it? My experiences are different from your experiences, so my "truth" can't be the same as your "truth," can it?

There are absolute truths that are unchangeable and irrefutable and can be debated and discussed, but the debate and the discussion won't change them.

Write down what you think are absolute truths.

_____
_____
_____
_____

Someone may have had a bad relationship experience and say all men are violent. That won't be true for the next person. They may seek out others who believe the same thing to validate their belief. Gathering more evidence doesn't make it true. They don't need to go very far to find evidence that men are kind and gentle.

So, what do you do when you find out your "truth" is not truth?

There are unseen forces all around you that want you to live with the untruths and to be stuck in places that stop your progression and to make your life miserable.

Funny thing about truth; truth has a frequency, so when we say, "Does that resonate with you?" It means, "Does that thing feel right or wrong to you?" Right would be a positive good

How to See and Recognize Truth

reaction. Wrong would be a negative or bad reaction. Frequencies don't lie.

So, you can conduct an experiment if you want to feel the difference.

Say this out loud, "I am loved."

Depending on your beliefs around that statement, it will either resonate with a good, positive feeling or a with bad, negative feeling.

Now say, "I am a worthless piece of garbage."

Even if this is a belief you have, it should always generate a negative or bad feeling.

If both of these statements generated a negative reaction. Write down a statement that you know will resonate positively with you so you will have a reference point for future experiences.

I am _____ (write a positive statement here).

If "I am loved" left you with a negative or bad feeling, your body is giving you a clue that something isn't right. You are holding a belief that isn't serving you. It is covering up who you truly are.

Keep reading and there will be ideas presented that will help you do this.

Seth

You might be feeling some resistance to all of this. Change can be daunting. It might help if you put your truth glasses on.

Let me tell you about truth glasses, spectacles, or lenses. There are pure. They carry no baggage from the past, no wounds, no confusion, no agenda, and no hidden meanings. They simply help you see the truth. So, for your first lesson in how to use truth glasses. You put them on and close your eyes and say a statement you know to be true for you. When you first put them on, they may be blurry but don't throw them away. It is your perception that made them blurry, not the glasses.

Now, how do you get a set of these truth glasses? For our purposes you can put on the glasses on the following page. One size fits all.

How to See and Recognize Truth

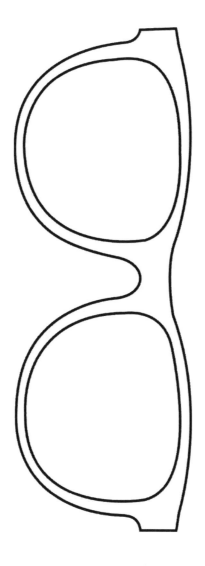

FOR YOU: A Guide to the Universe

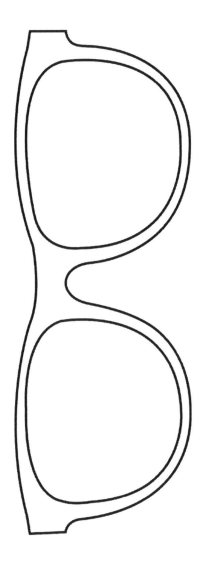

How to See and Recognize Truth

Your glasses are on. Your eyes are shut. You said your truth statement out loud. Now open your eyes. Look around and see if your vision has changed. Keep these glasses on for one day.

Record what you "see" differently:

_____
_____
_____
_____

If "I am loved" resonated negatively with you, repeat the exercise outlined above. Say, "I am loved." You can even write the words on the inside of the glasses and see what happens throughout the day. Feel free to substitute a different "I am" statement that resonated negatively with you for the "I am loved" statement.

Record what happens.

_____
_____
_____
_____

If you feel resistance that usually means you are tapped into something you are holding onto that you don't need any more.

Keep putting on the glasses until that true statement, the positive one you've chosen, can be "seen" through clear glasses. If you still can't see the truth clearly keep reading. There are other ways to see the truth.

Royce

I had a problem seeing truth. I was so beaten down by life that I had no hope of ever feeling good again or of having anything good in my life. I wasn't sure why I kept getting out of bed every morning. Sometimes I didn't. Pretty soon people just left me alone. Nothing they tried made any difference.

One night I was dozing off in front of the television and I saw myself dressed in nice clean clothes with a smile on my face and a fresh haircut and shave. I was talking to a group of people who had asked for directions. As they walked off, I continued on my way to my new job in an office. The office was a busy place. People smiled at me and greeted me like a friend. Wow! Then I saw myself walk to my decent car and drive home to a clean, well-cared for house. No peeling paint or weeds for grass and overflowing trash. Wow!

Inside the house was a family that was excited I was home. Children greeted me with a hug and a kiss, and my wife did the same. Wow! I was astonished.

Waking up from dozing off, I found myself still in front of the television surrounded by reminders that there was no hope. But, as I sat pondering, I could feel a change taking place. As I internalized the truth about who I really was and what kind of life I could have, I surprised myself by cleaning up the whole apartment. And it didn't stop there. I wrote down all I had seen of the life I could have, so I wouldn't forget.

You won't believe it, but I lived that life. My family is here with me now, in the place we go after we die. I am that person. The one I saw and truly am.

Harold

The truth was hard for me to see for most of my life. I wanted to see it, but I had decided it was too much work to try. The problem was I knew what it was but chose to ignore it. There was this moment though that changed everything. I had heard the phrase many times in my life but had never let it settle.

"You can do better than this."

This time I really heard it, and nothing has been the same since. I quit my job. Found a way to start the business I had always dreamed about. Now I can help people in the same situation I was in. I have the personality and the skills to help them hear the truth of my words. The truth they have known all along.

Manuel

My folks were big on teaching us about how much God loved us. I can't remember a time I didn't know that I was loved by a Father in Heaven. If there was a Father there had to be a Mother too.

As I grew, I made mistakes. There are times I would be reassured by my parents that God still loved me and always would.

When my baby died, they reassured me again that He loves me, and that He loved my baby too.

"How could that be?" I pled. "How could He let this happen?" My heart was broken in so many pieces it would never be the same. How could He love me and take away my precious baby boy?

From the time I could speak I had been taught to pray to a loving God. After the death of my baby my prayers were different. I had so many questions that I never seemed to get answers to. I was angry, sad, heartbroken, and empty. But somewhere deep inside I knew He still loved me.

One day many months after my son's death I felt a spark of something come alive in me. I was ready to hear the truth. I couldn't see or accept it before because of my anger and sadness.

As I let the spark grow within me, I felt the love of that Father I had been taught about all my life. I knew He loved my baby boy too and that we would be reunited one day. I would be able to hold him in my arms again.

Oh, how my heart burst with joy at the knowledge I would hold him again. Up until this moment I hadn't let that register as truth. I was able to let go of the anger and sadness, which opened a space to be able to receive the truth. I was then able to go on with life, with joy, and the anticipation of a beautiful reunion with my precious baby boy.

Sally

Truth has a way of softening us. When we are resisting it, we become hardened. We resist what we know we need to do, or not

How to See and Recognize Truth

do, or change. This hardened way of living creates tension in our bodies and affects other parts of us.

Pause for a moment. Take a deep slow breath in and exhale slowly and completely. Where are you holding tension in your body?

_____

_____

_____

_____

Sit with the tension for a moment. Focus on the area of your body you feel the tension in and see if you can get it to soften. Keep finding places holding tension and focus on them to soften until you come to one that won't soften. Take another deep breath in and out and sit with that place until it tells you something.

Record below what comes up.

_____

_____

_____

_____

As the truth comes to the surface you will feel that part that held the tension soften, which allows everything around it to soften as well.

In the future, when you feel tension in your body, whether it is in your jaw, or your gut for instance, breathe, focus on the place that is tense and wait for the truth to come up.

It may be that you truly are safe and don't need to be fearful. Or it could be that person's opinion of you truly does not matter and you are okay with however you are or with whatever you said. You may also need to fix something with an apology because you did say something that was untrue and the tension in your body will remain until you do what you need to do to release it.

Trust your truth!

Barstow

I have a story to tell and it's a good one. It happened when I wasn't looking. All my life I had thought that everyone saw the world as I did. It wasn't until I lost my dog that I realized what I saw was not what other people saw.

My dog was my best friend. He went with me everywhere he was allowed and some places he wasn't. When I slept, he slept. When I ate, he ate. Some people wondered if I would ever date. It's like we were more than best friends. As he got older, he slowed down a bit. We moved out and got our own apartment. He helped me with my homework by laying on my feet and keeping them warm.

I could see in his eyes that it was time for him to go and he knew it. He was worried about me, about leaving me alone. I just held him and whispered comforting things to him. It was during one of these quiet moments that he just slipped away.

At first, I panicked a little wondering what to do, but then I calmed down, laid him on his favorite blanket and took him home to the house and family we grew up in. We had a little ceremony in the backyard. There were a lot of tears. I didn't want to go back

How to See and Recognize Truth

to our empty apartment, but eventually I did. So many pictures, reminders of him and me, were everywhere. To this day I feel a warmth on my feet that is not coming from my socks.

I couldn't see it then, but I see it so clearly now. We all have someone that is part of us. Some of us have other things that are part of us. Some dogs are mean, and some people are mean.

We were part of each other because I needed him, and he needed me, and we were good for each other. He taught me what love was and I reciprocated. This would have been a very different story if I would have thought of him as just a hairy dog. And we both knew he was so much more than that.

I have a husband and children now and the warmth on my feet reminds me to look past what's on the outside and feel the truth that's on the inside.

Patrice

I have watched people come and go through the passage of time. My assignment has been to be available when called upon to help when the world is in chaos. The chaos has been steady for a very, very, long time.

Sometimes I wonder if I am helping at all. But occasionally people realize that the help they received came from an unseen source. I think people have lost hope. The darkness is crushing. There are bad things happening all around. The dark feels bigger than the light. Who do you trust?

Sit very still. Take a deep slow breath and then let it out. Close your eyes. Get very quiet inside. See yourself and then just wait. Can you see us? We are all around you and there is more than you can count. We are the good guys. There are more of us, the good guys, than the bad guys. You just can't see us.

The earth has been cleansed from time to time, but next time the cleansing will be complete. Please know we are here. We are doing what we can to mitigate the darkness. You can ask for help. You have angels assigned to you specifically and they are always there. But there are others, like me, that come when you call for help. It is a privilege and honor to help you.

Percival

Children are so good at speaking the truth. It comes naturally. They are learning about filters. If you have an opportunity, take some time and listen to their conversations. They are pure and unencumbered by what they should and should not say. It is best to do when they don't know anyone is listening.

One of the most profound conversations I have ever heard in my life was when I overheard the prayer of my five-year-old niece. She had been taught to talk to God her whole life. It seemed to come naturally to her. She was kneeling by her bed with her little hands clasped. Her eyes were closed, and she looked like she was concentrating very hard. I missed the beginning of her prayer, but this is what I heard.

I do love her.

I don't know why I am mean to her sometimes.

Will you help me be nicer?

My mom wants me to be nicer but sometimes I hear a voice tell me I hate her. She is ugly. I don't say those things, but I hear them. What should I do? The voice scares me.

How to See and Recognize Truth

You are sending someone?
Good, who is it?
I have an angel?
I have lots of angels?
So, what do I do when I hear the voice?
I stand up!
I say, go away!
What do I do next?
I remember you love me.
I remember I love her.
I remember she loves me.
I can do that.
Thank you.
I love you.
Goodnight.
Amen.

She got into bed. I came in and tucked her in. I told her goodnight and went to bed pondering how that conversation touched me. Her innocence. Her faith. Her trust. It seemed she was being spoken to and could hear Him. That she knew He was listening and that He could help her. There were no adults to prompt or interfere. I was never the same. I now have conversations with Him too. I remember He loves me. I love Him and I have angels to help me when I need them.

Macee

governments, your wars, your economics, and sometimes your hearts.

I wonder why you think you are here. When do you take time to connect with the God that made you, whose power it is that made this world and gives you breath?

If you haven't recently or ever slowed down long enough to say hello or thanks, can you do so now?

If you can't say it out loud could you write it?

_____

_____

_____

_____

Then get quiet and listen for the response. You may hear words. You may feel something small or big in your heart. If nothing comes please wait a little longer. Hold onto the words you spoke or wrote. If nothing comes, please try again. Try until you feel or hear something. He is there. He is always there. Don't forget about Him. You need Him now more than ever before. I have seen what's coming.

Chartu

My father and mother were kind of tough on me. They loved me but it was hard to be their kid. After I left home and raised my family, I was beat up emotionally. Being a parent was harder than I could have imagined. When I look back at my childhood, I realize that their toughness was their way of helping me to become a good person.

I tried hard with my own kids, but they all seem to hate me. I realize now what they needed was to be loved. More love always but toughness when it was needed.

I hope it's not too late to ask forgiveness and do better.

Samuel

The hawk is a most beautiful creature. Have you ever looked closely at their piercing eyes? They see everything. They are calculating, measuring and sensing. Their beaks are sharp. Their talons are sharp. They are swift and strong.

To calm them we use a hood. We take away their ability to see, to sense, to calculate and to function. We tie a piece of leather around their leg to keep them grounded and close to us.

Do we do that to the people around us? Do we take away their ability to see and function?

When you take the hood off a hawk their eyes are still piercing. Their beak and talons are still sharp. Does this happen to you? Do you put a "hood" over your head? Do you keep yourself grounded and stuck?

What aren't you seeing because of your "hood" and "tether"?

_____
_____
_____
_____

How are you "hooding" and "tethering" someone?

Could it be because you don't want to be seen? Could it be because you don't want to see the truth about yourself or others?

Observe a hawk in flight. Watch it closely. Let it teach you what it means to be free, to see the truth.

Persephone

I was a regular normal, everyday person. There was nothing extraordinary about me. Then there was this one day. I had come home from work. My dinner was in the oven. I was reading one of my favorite books when I just started crying. I was nothing like these interesting people on the pages. My life was boring, nothing to write about. I put the book down and fell onto my bed and sobbed for I don't know how long. My food was burned. I had no other ideas for dinner, and I didn't want to eat anyway. The sun went down and I didn't bother to turn the lights on. I sat in the dark for a long time.

How to See and Recognize Truth

I thought my life was complete. Routine, boring, and solid, but complete.

"So why was I crying and so upset?" I asked myself, never expecting to get an answer.

There's more.

"More what?" I said out loud.

More to you than you think there is.

Then I got a little freaked out.

"Who are you and where is this coming from?"

I turned the lights on.

No one.

I got a drink of water.

Then I thought it couldn't hurt to ask, "You said there was more to me. What does that mean?"

What have you always wanted to do but don't think you can justify it?

"Well that's easy, learn to paint."

There you go. More of you.

"What?"

You are an artist, that's why you have wanted to paint. What have you always secretly dreamed about?

"Being a nurse."

Are you a nurse now?

"No."

Why not?

"Lots of reasons."

That's more of you.

I was starting to feel a little hungry and so I made myself a sandwich. I asked the person speaking, "Do you want one." Just to be polite.

No thank you.

I sat at the kitchen table pondering this "more of me." Eventually I said, "What's your point?"

No point. Just having a conversation.

After my sandwich was eaten, I realized how tired and worn out I felt and shuffled to my bed.

The next morning as I opened my eyes, the sunlight coming through the curtains looked different. My clothes felt different on my body. My usual morning beverage tasted better than normal. When I got home that night I looked around, halfway expecting someone to be sitting on my sofa.

Just for fun, I will stop by the college to see what I would have to do to get a nursing degree.

I also noticed a twinkle in my eye that wasn't there before. Maybe that is "more of me." I plan to find out.

Geraldine

There is a precious part of each of you that is most sacred, most holy, and most pure. It is who you truly are. As you journey through life you pick up stuff along the way that interferes with how you see yourself. So how do you get to the true you? And why would you want to?

The true you is unencumbered by those things that someone told you, that you heard, and the things you have felt that were degrading and negative that made you question your worth.

God sees your true self. He always has and always will. He sees through all of what isn't truly you.

How to See and Recognize Truth

Ask to see who you truly are through His eyes, to see and feel His love for you.

Record the answer:

_____
_____
_____

In that love is hope. Hope that you will do what you need to do to become what you always were. To let go of all that is holding you in the past and embrace what is now.

You are hardwired to do this. You are not alone in this transformation, this remembering. Be patient but diligent. Gentle with yourself, but persistent. Always with the hope and expectation of discovering the true you.

Who do you want that true you to be?

_____
_____
_____

Betty

★ ✹ ★

I was born into a family that loved and feared God. We lived in the woods far away from other people. We lived off the land

and any off jobs my father or mother could scrounge up. I never would have known how poor we were if I had never left home. I only went to the next town, but my eyes were opened. A kind man gave me a job and a cot to sleep on in the back of his store.

Eventually my clothing got better, my appearance brightened up some and my verbal skills improved. But, I felt, for the first time, that God was missing from my life. Life was simpler back home. We made time to talk to God and He talked back.

It was so easy to see God all around us back home. He was in the breeze, the snow, the trees, the turkeys, the fish, the water and my family. That was what was missing. I don't know how the townspeople got on without Him. You didn't have to be wealthy to have it and you didn't need to be poor either, though it seemed easier to have Him in your life if you were poor, humble, and needy.

I missed how much God was a part of my life when I was with my family. Each day I try to make sure I feel His presence in my life. I never want to be without Him.

Can you see Him in your life?

_____

_____

_____

_____

He is all around you. If you can't see Him now, keep looking.

Cheryl

How to See and Recognize Truth

I was a stonecutter for the pharaohs of Egypt. I worked 44 years in their stone quarries. There would never be a grand pyramid built for me when I passed to the world beyond. I pondered many years on why that was so. I knew that pharaohs were gods and I definitely wasn't a god. But why all this work and preparation? If I tried to talk to someone else about my questions they would get upset and threaten to expose me to our superiors.

One night I had a dream in which I was walking through a lush garden. Beauty was everywhere around me. Other people would walk past me and acknowledge me with a head motion, a wave or a handshake and an introduction. Eventually I sat on a bench by a waterfall. I was so wrapped up in my thoughts I didn't notice someone sat down next to me.

By and by we began conversing and I learned he had been one of the pharaohs of Egypt. He asked where I was from and I froze in my spot. How could this be? He was a normal looking man and I would never have guessed he was anything more than an ordinary guy. When I finally found my words, I continued the conversation never letting on that I was in servitude to the pharaohs. I woke up with a start and laid there on my humble mat, pondering the dream.

Next thing I knew I was at work carving and cutting stones for someone like that man in my dream. I didn't dare share the dream with anyone. They already thought they should turn me in.

That night I went to bed, still pondering as I fell asleep.

My dream this night changed my life forever. I was back on the bench in the same garden. A person approached me and asked if I would please come with them. They seemed to be on an important errand, so I followed. The further we walked the brighter it got. I was aware of an awe and reverent feeling that seemed to be strong in this place.

The person I was following stopped and asked me to wait where I was. They were gone a few moments and then I saw them gesture to me to come to where they were. I came around the corner and as my eyes adjusted to the brilliant light, I saw the real and true Gods. I sank to my knees and bowed forward as low as I could go.

I wasn't sure I could look upon them. I knew somehow there was more than one. I could hardly breathe. I don't know how much time passed but I felt someone approach where I was on the floor. I felt a gentle touch on my head.

Slowly I raised my head to see and I beheld the most glorious being. He helped me to my feet and then embraced me. Enveloped me in His arms. I felt so many indescribable feelings in that moment. Time seemed to stand still. I heard a voice that pierced through to my soul say, "This is my beloved son. The God of this earth, the sky and the stars."

Oh, how I wish I could convey my thoughts and feelings in that moment. Those words, the light, the love, and the knowledge that these are real and true Gods.

I realized I had questions and they talked with me. It was as if time didn't exist. I asked what I was to do with this knowledge that I now had of them as true Gods when I returned to earth, my life, and my occupation in servitude? With this knowledge came a humble, deep love for all of mankind. Even though a pyramid would never be built for me I knew I was a child of a God and so was the pharaoh I served. We are all loved equally by the true God who I now serve. When my eyes opened, there I was back on my

How to See and Recognize Truth

humble mat, in my humble working quarters, as a stone cutter for the pharaohs.

Others asked about my countenance. They said I looked different. When I was allowed to go to my family, I felt the light grow within me as I shared bits and pieces of what I had learned with those who were prepared to hear.

When I passed from this life to the next, I was greeted by the God of this earth and the sky and the stars and so much more.

Teni

There have been times since the earth was created that wickedness and righteousness were prevalent. There have been moments when righteousness prevailed and moments when wickedness prevailed. Never has there been a time when both have prevailed at the same time.

They both are escalating as never before. Each person on the earth and in heaven will be required to choose either wickedness or righteousness. There is no neutral ground in this war.

How will you know the difference? The powers of wickedness would have you think they are righteous, in the right, justified, and persecuted and that the righteous are evil, misguided, wrong and the enemy.

How will you know?

The God who created you fitted you with a compass. One that you could rely on to point to the truth. The powers of darkness try to interfere with your compass. They try to move the lines, blur the lines, make counterfeit lines, remove the lines completely and to interfere with your ability to see the truth at all.

So, what can you do if you want to see what is truth and utilize the compass you were given? Where is this compass? How does it work? How do you know if it is working properly?

Next time you need to make a decision and don't know which is the right way and need and want to see the truth, pause. Get very still. Ask to see the compass in your mind's eye, your imagination, look for an arrow that is pointing up, like North. North represents truth. You can do a test. Think of something you know to be untrue and look at the arrow, the pointer. Where is it pointing to? Anything off of North, of the truth, is untruth or has untruth in it. Now think of something you know to be true and see where the arrow or pointer is now.

This is a visualization to help you feel what is truth and what is untruth. Eventually you won't need to see the pointer or arrow. You will be able to feel it in your body.

You have not been left alone here on the earth without the tools to see and know what is true. People on the earth at this time and in the future will need to be able to discern the truth from the untruth like they have never had to before.

The darkness knows what's coming and they are holding nothing back. But the light also knows what is ahead and everything in the light is available to those who desire it.

If you want to see clearly, to know how to protect yourself and your family and not be deceived into paths that bring not only heartache but death also, find your compass.

Learn what truth feels like.

How to See and Recognize Truth

What does your truth feel like?

___

___

___

___

Flemish

I lived in a time of great upheaval on the earth. Everything seemed to be in commotion. Many of the people around me gave into their fears and did horrible things.

Every day I prayed for protection for me and my family. We didn't dare leave our homes. Food was running out and we were all becoming very frightened. Hope seemed a fragile thing for all of us. It was late one evening when I knew we needed to leave. "How?" I asked. The streets weren't safe. For that matter nowhere was safe. The urgency to leave got stronger and stronger. So, I asked my family and those who were sheltered in my home, to pack only what they needed. The small amount of the food we had was distributed among all of us.

When all was ready, we knelt and asked for protection. Grateful for how we had been preserved until now. We trusted, that in acting on the knowing I had felt, that we would be blessed for doing as prompted, not knowing beforehand how it would all play out. We had no plan just a sliver of hope.

For many days we heard gunfire and screaming all around us. As we were praying, I knew which way we should leave the house. We talked to the children about how quiet they needed to be. They seemed to know already. Carefully I opened the door. It was so dark outside. It was decided that I would lead, and all would follow close in my footsteps. I sensed we weren't alone. There were unseen beings all around us.

I somehow knew how far to go forward, when to turn, which way to turn, and when to stop. At times we could hear people coming. All of us instinctively froze where we stood. But those who were running seemed not to see us. We continued, even though we could still hear gunfire, yelling, and terrified people.

Time seemed to stand still. The sun started appearing on the horizon. It was then I realized we had been walking all night. We found ourselves at a cave in the foothills. There were footsteps in the dirt. Whomever had been here was gone now. All 17 of us had made it to a safe place. We quietly thanked the Lord for making the miracle of our preservation possible. We observed people walking by the entrance to the cave, but they didn't seem to notice we were there. After we were all rested, I felt like it was time to go. I didn't know where. I dared to let myself hope for our deliverance to a safe place. On our knees we asked for protection again. Again, I led, and they followed. Again, unseen beings accompanied us. We walked through the night.

As the sun rose the next morning, I realized we had crossed into a valley I had been to before. Someone I knew and trusted lived in this valley. We made our way there and with great faith I knocked on her door and was greeted with open arms. I asked if we could stay with her until we could make other arrangements. She looked surprised and said she didn't have room for everyone.

I turned to look at our little band of refugees. I told her of our number and again she looked surprised. "But I see a multitude of people," she whispered.

How to See and Recognize Truth

As I looked again at my family and friends, my eyes were opened and I saw what she saw. Standing all around us there were soldiers with shields and weapons. My family and friends saw them too. Then they began to disappear one by one. We knew now why no one seemed to see us or sense our presence. The soldiers had been there the whole time. Words escaped me.

She did have room for us, and we never forgot the soldiers and our safe deliverance from evil and darkness.

My faith was tested in those extreme and dangerous circumstances. I know we aren't ever alone. I know they are there watching and in our need they will come to our aid.

So, be brave and have courage. Trust in what you can't see, and you will be led, protected, and delivered from darkness and evil.

Susannah

FOR YOU: A Guide to the Universe

NOTES

CHAPTER 7

The Lies

I grew up being told I was wicked and a sinner. I believed the adults in my life telling me this because they believed they were wicked and sinners too. It wasn't because of anything I had done wrong. I was a good girl. It never made sense to me.

I began to question the truth of this belief and was treated as even more wicked and sinful. It made no sense. Somewhere inside I knew they were wrong. So began my pursuit of what was true about me.

In college I listened to fellow students and professors answer my question as to whether we were wicked and sinners or not. I got so many opinions and answers I didn't feel like I was getting anywhere. For a time, I stopped asking. Then a miracle happened.

I met a man at the grocery store I shopped at. One day as I was shopping and deep in thought, he approached me and asked what I was thinking about. His question took me by surprise. It seemed I was always deep in thought. Before I knew it, I had told him of my question and how none of the answers and opinions I had received had made sense to me.

He smiled and said, "I know who you are. Sometimes we make wicked and sinful choices but that doesn't change the truth that you are a daughter of a powerful, loving, kind, Heavenly Father who knows you and loves you no matter what you do that is wicked or sinful. He wants you to be happy. He wants you to return one day to live with Him again."

I was frozen, speechless, couldn't believe I was hearing what I was hearing, because I felt it all over my body. Everything was tingling like I was electrified. He just stood there smiling and waiting for me to recover from the shock.

I blurted out, when I finally found my voice, "How do you know this?"

"I once thought the same thing that you did. That I didn't have a chance to be good because I was, and would always be, wicked and a sinner. So, I chose to be a sinner and did wicked things. What did I have to lose? I was already going to hell, why not enjoy the journey.

"But the whole time I knew this wasn't me. It felt wrong. It felt off. It wasn't me. I moved. I changed jobs. I started a new life to get away from the wicked and sinful life I had been living. I wanted to know who I truly was. That is the look I saw on your face as you were trying to pick out some produce."

I could hardly wait for the rest of his story. "Look into your heart," he said.

"How do I do that?" I asked him.

"You came to the earth with the truth inside you. You were also born with the results of the life experiences of all of those whose blood runs in your veins. You might think of that as starting your life experience with a disadvantage. Along with the negative came the positive. The weaknesses with the strengths. But always and forever with the truth inside of you."

"So, you aren't going to tell me how to find this truth? You just wanted me to know it is there?" I questioned.

He said, "If I tell you, it won't have the same impact that you, finding it out yourself, will have."

I thanked him, bought my groceries, and left the store.

I couldn't get what he had said out of my mind. I didn't want to talk to anyone about our conversation. They were content to accept the teachings they had grown up with and their parents and grandparents and so on. One night I was alone and still pondering, wondering and frustrated, "How was I to find this truth?"

An angel appeared in front of me. She was smiling and beautiful. There was no reason for me to be afraid. She slowly leaned towards me and softly touched her finger to where my heart is. She whispered, "You will find your answers here," then as she gestured to my head, "not here."

I was alone again, but now I felt something growing. It was as if the containers, the truth was imprisoned in, were cracking and breaking as this knowing was growing. I don't know how long it took but the cracking finally stopped. It is as if I could see into my soul and what I saw took my breath away.

I saw purity. I saw beauty. I saw goodness. I saw a beautiful clean woman full of joy, and the light that shone all around her was intoxicating. I knew it was me. I knew it was who I truly am, and I knew I was loved in a way I had never imagined.

As that incredible vision of my true self dissipated, I could feel my body tingling from head to foot. Almost like I was being rebooted, reset, purged, electrified, empowered and renewed.

I stayed still until the resetting completed itself. I stood up and felt different all over, inside and out. I wrote down this experience in detail. I felt like I had stepped from the darkness into the light.

I understood why the man at the grocery store hadn't told me what is was, but where to find it and you can too. You will not have the same experience as I did but whatever experience you have will be intimately suited to you and you alone.

I know who I am and that has made all the difference.

Cecily

Through all generations of time the human body has been either respected or abused. There seems to have been a lot of confusion surrounding its purpose. Across cultures and religions there are differing rules or opinions about how much of the body can be exposed and what should be covered up. Each person has come to this earth because a physical body was created for their spirit to dwell in.

Our spirits were limited as to what they could do. Combined with a physical body our opportunities to grow and experience life were magnified. The powers of darkness would have you believe that your body is for a one time use only, so get as much mileage out of it as you can.

The truth is your body will be part of your eternity, which is a very long time. Your body is also a place where records are kept of whatever your body has experienced, felt, seen or heard. All your words and thoughts have been recorded.

How to See and Recognize Truth

This information may make you uncomfortable. You might say that's not possible. You might panic a little thinking that no one will know what you have done in secret so what does it matter. Your physical body is a gift from a loving Father in Heaven who will require an accounting, at a later time, with what you did with it. You won't have to speak. He will see it in the records you carry in that body of yours. All your doings, thoughts, words and feelings, good and bad, will determine where you go next. Your body is a gift, what you do with it or to it is your gift to the creator. Choose wisely.

Marie

When I was a little girl my grandmother told me about a friend of hers who talked a lot. She thought the friend was a bit weird and didn't really give any credence to the stories she told. She was sure her friend made them all up. But there was one story her friend had shared that my grandmother couldn't seem to forget. It kind of haunted and bothered her. She resisted the thought that it might be true and wanted to just forget it and go on with her life.

This was the story:

"I always thought we were on our own when it came to decisions we would have to make. You know the big life-altering decisions and, for that matter, the small decisions too.

"But I noticed something interesting as I made decisions. It seemed like doors would open when I was going in the right direction. Other times I would get little nudges to gently steer myself onto a different path. Then I began noticing the feeling I had each time a decision was to be made. One day, after getting comfortable with this little system that had manifested with my decision-making process, I ended up making a decision that set me on a downward spiral that I didn't think I could recover from. What about my beautiful system that had been working so well? How did it all go wrong?

"Then, I was afraid to make any decisions. I was paralyzed with fear, doubt, anger, and sadness. My self-confidence was gone. I didn't know what to do.

"Then one day I felt a little whisper. It said: '"I want you to be happy. I want you to succeed in life. I want you to know you are loved and you are not alone. I open those doors. I send gentle nudges. I am there even if your decision takes you away from me. Just ask for help and I will be there.'

"I felt hope trickle back into my heart, so I asked for help from the whisper. Soon the trickle was a roaring river. My spiral reversed and with gratitude I celebrated the knowledge I have that we are not alone. There is a powerful being that wants the best for me and for you. We just need to ask."

Her story changed my life. I now know the whisperer.

Sarah

The powers of darkness want us to feel isolated from everyone else.

I can do things on my own.

I don't need any help.

I can figure it out myself.

How to See and Recognize Truth

I am not hurting anyone.

This is about me.

No one knows what I have been through.

No one understands what I am going through.

The list is endless. We close ourselves off thinking we are the odd one out. The truth is, we are all connected. We are here to help each other through this mortal journey.

There is someone who has been where you are and has experienced what you are going through. Reach out. Ask for help. Don't let the darkness keep you down and suffering.

Frank

I lived in a small remote village for most of my life. I was loved and fed and taken good care of. We worked hard as a family and were very close to each other. One day I was sent to a neighboring village to get some supplies. While I was there, we all felt a rumbling in the earth beneath our feet. I got what I needed and then started back to my village. As I got closer there was so much dust in the air.

I could have traveled the path to my village with my eyes closed I knew it so well. Eventually I had to stop because there were boulders and rocks that littered the trail. I began to feel worried. I knew something terrible had happened. I tried to climb over the boulders but lost the path. I knew I had to wait until I could see, until the dust settled.

Soon others were trying to see where the rumbling came from. When the dust settled, we could see what had caused the rumbling and all the rocks and boulders. Some of the nearby mountain was missing, like it had been sliced off. The village and all my people were buried under the pieces of the mountain. Some of us finally got to where the village should have been. There were no sounds. We called and called hoping to find survivors. There was no response. With a heart heavy filled with sorrow I made my way slowly and numbly back to the village I had gone to for supplies.

Why would God do this to my family and all those people? Why would He leave me all alone? The elders of the village met to determine what was to be done with me. I was assigned to work for a family in their village in exchange for a place to sleep. No one could answer my questions. Why would God do this? Many days went by. Weeks and months passed. The family was kind to me, and I worked very hard for them.

A strange man came to the village one day. He said he was looking for the survivor of the rock avalanche. I was found and delivered to him.

He listened to my story and to my questions. He then told me he had been sent by God to find me. He had a message from God for me.

"Some would have you believe your family and the village were being punished for their wickedness and you know that is not true. Some would have you believe there is no answer and God is mean and unfeeling.

"I am here to tell you that you were spared to tell the story of your village and your family. He knew you would be strong. He knew you would wonder why. He loves you. He blessed you to be strong and to be able to love and be kind even though your heart was broken.

How to See and Recognize Truth

"He is not a vindictive, vengeful, mean, spiteful God. The villagers and your family are with Him. So, be of good cheer. You will see them again. Record their history so they aren't forgotten. You have a work to do. That is why you were spared."

He looked into my eyes and gently squoze my hands. Then he was gone.

My heart misses them but is no longer broken for them. There is purpose and gratitude in my life now. I went on to record all I could remember about my village, my family, and the merciful God that watches over all of us.

Chimea

The powers of darkness would have you believe in them. They want you to believe that you are important to them. You are important to them, but not for the reasons you think. My father used to tell me not to trust in things that felt too easy. That didn't make much sense when I was young, but life has shown me the truth in his teaching.

The darkness uses "easy" to hook you and before you know it you are doing their work for them. Bad is sugar coated with good sometimes. But you don't see at first what is just under the sugar coating.

With the hook comes enticing words. Words that would have you think that it's not so bad. No one needs to know. It's just this once. But now they know your weaknesses and they won't stop until you do it again, again and again. They want you to forget all that is good and wholesome. All that brought you true joy.

They make you think this will make you happy and when you are so far in, they abandon you. They have fed off watching you fall into their snare and they would have you think you are too far in to get out.

Those that truly care about you warn you about what is happening. They try to help but you will have none of it. Your new "friends" have all you need. You've got this. Only when you lose all that once mattered to you, and your new "friends" get what they want and abandon you, do you hear your dad's words and fully understand what they meant.

Then what do you do? Your mind and your body and your soul are shredded, empty, gutted, and without strength. No one trusts you; they are afraid of you and there is no hope. Death seems like a sweet release from the hell you now find yourself in.

Somewhere, buried deep under all the hooks and aftermath, lies a small seed. In the darkness you can see the seed. You feel its warmth, you feel its love. How could something good still be there in all the darkness? How do you know it is a good seed?

You don't trust yourself anymore. You try to ignore it. But instead of disappearing it gets a little warmer. Sometimes, you sit with the seed and just feel its warmth and love. You know now it is not going away. It is your evidence that there is hope and you know there is a power of light that knows you and wants you to live. Not just live for the sake of living, but live with more light and love and warmth than you thought was possible.

Those "new friends" of yours sense a change in you and that they might be losing you to the light. That is when they pull out all the stops to kill the seed forever. They make it look so easy, so simple, so enticing.

How to See and Recognize Truth

The seed is fighting for you but can only grow if you choose the light. No one can choose this for you. It is up to you.

Where does the strength come from to choose the light and turn your back on the darkness? It comes from the seed. That beautiful, little, powerful, warm seed that is within you. Just stop and feel its warmth envelop you. Allow it to grow. It is stronger than all of those "new friends," stronger than all the darkness, strong enough to pull you out of the darkness and into the light.

Will you let it?

Marshall

My mother always told me I was beautiful, and I believed her. Sometimes when others told me I was beautiful they had different reasons for saying it than my mother had. I often felt uncomfortable.

Being beautiful began to take up a lot of my time and I thought a lot about it. Some people were shocked or disappointed when they saw me when I wasn't as perfectly beautiful as they expected me to be. I started to rebel a bit and gained a little weight just to see what would happen.

Some people stopped paying me any attention. Others commented on how I had let myself go. Others were disappointed.

So I wondered what beauty was. Was it perfection? Should it require so much time? Was my beauty what attracted them or was it who was behind the beauty? What about me, my substance, who I was? Who was I beautiful for? Who decided what looks beautiful and what wasn't?

I had to do a lot of soul searching. I had enjoyed the attention. But when I found out that some of it was because of the outside not the inside, I was disillusioned by it all. I wanted to be pretty. I wanted to be beautiful. I didn't want to be ugly just to prove a point.

I began to observe people around me of all shapes, sizes, colors and walks of life. I watched the attention some people were given and those that weren't. How they carried themselves. Whether they looked confident or like they were trying to be invisible. I came to a conclusion I wasn't expecting.

Beauty and perfection in our physical form dictates for most people how they show up in life. It affects their relationships with others, including their relationship with themselves. It made me sad as I observed so much time and money spent on hiding flaws and imperfections. For what? to be accepted, to be loved, to be important?

I began to focus on the beauty I hoped I had inside. And as I did, I felt a beauty not born of perfection but of authenticity. The more I connected with who I truly was, the more beautiful I felt all over.

How beautiful do you feel? When you look in the mirror, what do you see?

_____

_____

_____

_____

How to See and Recognize Truth

You are inherently beautiful inside and out. If you don't feel that it is because you are listening to all those voices that want you to believe there is a standard for beauty that you will never meet but that you should always strive for.

Listen to your own internal compass, which is an expert on your individual beauty. Follow where it points to. Be the most beautiful you, you can be.

Ferrah

It has been said that truth is based on someone's life experience and that one person's truth is different from the next person's. Some would have you believe truth is fluid and changes as it needs to, to fit the person, the culture, the season or the current need.

How do you tell the difference between a universal truth and an untruth? Why do we need to know the difference?

First, if we are on a path or journey based on untruths, our path or journey won't help us reach our destination. Instead we will find ourselves somewhere that we never intended to be.

Untruths are meant to distract us from our true purpose. Untruths waste our precious time. If you built a house or assemble a piece of furniture with materials that represent untruths your house will collapse, and the pieces of furniture won't fit together. Sometimes the untruths are mixed with truths which creates a whole other level of materials that don't fit together properly.

If you are guided by truths on your journey you will reach the destination you were meant to. If untruths are your guide you won't reach the destination you wanted.

How can you tell if words, thoughts, beliefs, or directions are truths or untruths? You look at their fruits. Fruits, meaning their words, their thoughts, their beliefs or their direction.

Do the words take you to a place that feels right, good and productive? Do the thoughts ring true to your soul? Do the beliefs help you down your intended path or off into places of distraction or chaos? Do the directions bring order or chaos and confusion?

When truths are your guiding principles, the house you are building fits together correctly and the result is a beautiful, well made, strong, and safe dwelling. The furniture pieces all fit together with the result being a comfortable, functional, beautiful piece of furniture.

You always have a choice as to which type of path or journey you want to travel on.

Choose wisely!

Torrence

In the moment, you can feel a truth open up to you in a powerful and undeniable way. When the moment has passed, your confidence in that truth starts to waver. It is later that the questioning and doubt come in. Why is this so? Is it because passion is fleeting and so is truth? Is it because you were misled and what you thought was the truth was actually a lie?

There are forces that would have you doubt everything you hear, read, or know for the purpose of thwarting your purpose and mission here on earth.

One of their greatest tools to accomplish their goals is doubt. It may seem like a small insignificant word, but it can be extremely destructive and unravel the very foundation of who you are and who you are striving to become.

Doubt crushes confidence. It stops you in your tracks. It makes you question your every move. It also causes you to rethink your initial decision, the one that felt so good and so right at the time. So, what do you do when the seed of doubt is planted in your heart and mind? You go back to the original moment when you felt the truth of that word or thought. It might help to record these moments when they are fresh in your mind. Because time passes and you do start to forget the details. If others felt the same thing at the same time, let them help you remember. Trust that your feelings in that moment were real and from the ultimate source of truth. Then, watch for the fruits. If they are sweet and good, then it is truth. If the fruits are bitter, then it was an untruth.

Sometimes these feelings are very subtle and you have to be vigilant about seeing them. With practice you will know what truth feels like, so practice. Be aware of the subtle clues all around you every day. They are there and will guide you to the truth. Look for them, expect them, and express gratitude for them when they come.

Bartholomew

I thought life was supposed to be easy when I was doing everything right. So if something wasn't easy, I must be doing something wrong. Many times I would evaluate what I did that was wrong. I made it about me instead of about life as it naturally unfolded. I felt like I was responsible for the difficulties.

One day out of frustration I proclaimed my independence from doing life wrong all the time. When I had calmed down enough to think clearly, I thought long and hard about what was really happening when my life became difficult.

Something very interesting occurred. It was as if blinders were taken off my eyes and I could clearly see that life was just happening like it always had and always would. With some courage I anticipated there would soon be another difficult moment or event in my life, and I was determined to see it with my new eyes.

I acknowledge some difficulties were of my own making, but the ones brought on by simply being alive, I hoped would look different to me. Sure enough, a few days later a coworker brought something potentially difficult to my attention. Instead of taking responsibility for the mess, my new way of seeing kicked in and a solution presented itself and life went on.

It worked! I felt like I had discovered gold, hidden treasure, pirate loot, the fountain of youth. With my new eyes the whole world seemed a bit brighter, people a bit nicer, and I felt a lot stronger. No more self-defeating ways of looking at a situation.

Take responsibility for what is yours and see the rest for what it truly is. Check your glasses and see which ones you are wearing when life seems to be too much to bear. Find your part. Resolve it if you can. Embrace life as one of your greatest teachers.

Perry

How to See and Recognize Truth

As a nurse I see all kinds of people as patients along with those that support them. Through the years I have watched people turn their very lives over to the medical personnel assigned to them. I have also watched as patients take responsibility for their health and ask questions and get involved in their care, if they are capable of doing so.

There are those that would have you believe that you can't know your own body, that your body is evil, that it is something to be feared, shunned, or punished.

I see the physical body as a miraculous, magnificent, miracle. I try to help patients, and anyone I meet, recognize and remember the gift their bodies are. You do have power over what caused the illness, how you feel about the illness, and what actions you will take to return your body to a state of health and strength.

Age isn't a factor in this way of seeing your body. You probably will need some help and guidance as you become aware and learn about what you can do. The help and helpers are out there. Ask for help. Express your desire to master your body and learn how to support it. Watch then for doors to be opened and for helpers to be put on your path. With gratitude, act on your newfound knowledge and expect a healthier, happier life. Then share the message of what you have learned and empower others with what you now have.

Jana

Simply put, lies are meant to throw you off track. They are easy to detect sometimes and hard, if not impossible, to detect at other times. They hide the truth.

Why would the truth need to be hidden? To protect someone? To spare their feelings? To avoid a fight? To make you look better? To manipulate someone or a situation? To be accepted?

What is the alternative? Danger, hurt feelings, loneliness, fights, ostracism, or mediocrity; or someone liking, accepting, or including you without the lies?

When you tell a lie, the light that emanates from you will shrink. Why is this significant? It is very difficult to make good decisions, to function in a healthy way in a relationship, and to be yourself when lies are involved.

Some might say lying is necessary to keep the peace, to protect family, or to navigate a career. When is the truth better than one of these lies? With every choice comes a consequence and with every lie comes the need to continue lying to keep up the false reality that the lies create. It is exhausting and eventually you slip up and get caught in your lies. The consequences of getting caught in a lie is usually worse than the truth would have been in the beginning.

A lie many people buy into is that "no one will know." But you know, and God knows.

You have a choice, pick truth. At first it may not seem like you made the right choice, but in the long run you will be glad you did. So will those you are truthful with.

Jardine

I come as a messenger from the Most High God with a warning for you: There will come a day of reckoning where you will stand before Him and make an accounting of your actions,

How to See and Recognize Truth

your thoughts, and your deeds while on this earth. This is not negotiable.

I leave you my witness that this is an undeniable truth.

Thomas

FOR YOU: A Guide to the Universe

NOTES

CHAPTER 8

Steps to Take to Return Home

My folks were very busy people. They didn't have a lot of time for religion. But they made sure we said our prayers every day. They taught us how to pray when we were very young. We always knew God was listening.

But I grew up and stopped praying because it seemed childish to me at the same time.

Then one day I found myself talking to Him about something that was really bothering me. I felt peace and comfort wash over me, along with some ideas about how to solve my problem. If you don't pray, try it.

Harry

Family, it's what it's all about. We are born into connection. Sometimes the connections are tenuous and not always set in stone. We were meant to share, cry, celebrate, laugh and support each other. If we don't have family, we look for it in different places. If your family connections are strong and healthy, keep up the good work. If those connections are unstable or non-existent, maybe it's time to do some healing.

What connection in your life needs some healing?

_____
_____
_____
_____

Sinead

It really is about the small and simple things. Kindness is one of those small but powerful simple things. It means you are looking around outside of yourself. Kindness is selfless, it may be small and simple to you but to the receiver it can be life changing and life renewing.

So be on the lookout. You never know who may appear on your radar needing a kind gesture, smile, or some sweet words of encouragement.

Damian

Nature is known to have "magical" properties that seem to fill us up when we are running low. To give us a boost when we need a little more to get the juices flowing. Nature provides a place to connect with your higher power. That connection seems to be closer and more accessible to you when you are on a mountain path, splashing through the waves, or in the middle of a fragrant meadow.

There is power and stillness in these places. Make time to feel the stillness and plug into the power.

Mattias

If the eyes are the windows to the soul, it shouldn't be hard to spot the souls who are struggling. "What then?" You might ask. "Why me? I don't know what to do or what they need." Simply asking, "How can I help? What do you need? What can I do?" One of these questions might start a much-needed dialogue for healing their soul.

You can be a soul healer.

Paul

Laughter can cure many ills. There is something magical in a laugh. Every laugh is as unique as the person who is laughing. How long has it been since the sound of good laughter came from you? Those who have the gift of laughter are a precious commodity, especially for those who take life a bit too seriously.

Cerrano

You were born to be creative. When was the last time you built a sandcastle, changed a recipe to make it your own, or reorganized your humble, but adequate living quarters?

With creativity comes possibilities, the ability to see something in your mind and bring it to the physical world. Creating a beautiful life is also a creative act as you discover or bring together everything you will need for the life you desire. Being creative also includes the ability to adapt as needed.

What are you creating right now?

_____
_____
_____
_____

Bernard

Have you ever caught a frog, held onto a horse's mane or gathered a warm egg from under a chicken? Animals were created to populate the earth, bring us joy, help us work, and fill our bellies, among the long list of their many purposes.

Animals provide us with a connection that is unique to each species. A connection you might want to explore if you haven't yet. The rewards are wonderful.

Percival

Steps to Take to Return Home

Hard work is not only good for the body but is good for the spirit as well. Hard work can be found in the physical, mental, emotional and spiritual areas of your life. Some say hard work builds character along with the strong muscles. Hard work can be mentally strenuous as well when you have difficult problems to solve. Emotional hard work can include finding out what is causing your angry outbursts and working to heal what is bringing disharmony to your peace and happiness. Spiritual hard work is for the times you have questions about life.

Physically hard work seems to help you deal with the stresses of life and as a result your yard looks good too.

Smith

I once had a co-worker who stole from the company we worked for whenever he could. He felt justified because he thought he should have a higher salary. So he felt that the things he took from them made up the difference. I felt his actions were wrong no matter what rationalization he used.

Honesty is part of a strong character and will get you more places than dishonesty will. Dishonesty can be corrected by restoring what was taken, but that is not always an option.

Being honest with yourself is not always the easiest thing to do but is worth the effort.

Honesty brings peace of mind and a clean conscience, which is a much safer and stronger way to live.

Dennis

FOR YOU: A Guide to the Universe

Your word used to be as binding as a legal contract. The words you use can define you, speak volumes about what you believe, and share with others how you feel. On the other hand, your words can destroy, degrade, or hurt. Words can't be taken back. So, think before you speak and speak only the truth.

Salrout

★ ✹ ★

Music touches your soul. Music speaks to your feelings and connects those feelings to memories. Music is a powerful tool to set a mood which can be a sacred one or a frenzied one.

Whether you play one instrument or many, or just listen or dance to music, it affects you and whomever can hear it.

What do you listen to and why?

_____
_____
_____
_____
_____

Torrence

What are your gifts? Everyone has at least one. A gift is something you are naturally good at. Something that is part of who you are. You might have the gift of compassion or the gift of being able to speak in a way that is easily understood. Sometimes your gifts become evident later in your life. Any gift can be refined and honed. Additional gifts can be asked for if you feel you need or want them. Gifts not used will be lost.

What are your gifts?

_____

_____

_____

_____

Bertrand

Have you noticed that people see what they want to see usually?

It takes a humble and teachable person to see the truth, whether it be the truth under the words of an angry person, the truth behind tear-filled eyes, or the truth of your own deep sadness. If you want to see truth, ask to be able to do so. You might feel the urge to act on what you are shown. Be prepared to do so.

Menna

Gratitude is one of the most important qualities anyone can possess. Gratitude for what we have is a beginning that leads to gratitude for our trials. One might easily feel gratitude for blessings. It is difficult to see what you can be grateful for in the trial. It may seem counterintuitive to look for the blessing or the gift in the midst of heartache and pain. But that is where you will find the most exquisite opportunities for gratitude.

Sal

I wish that you would be ready and prepared for what is coming. A man protects his home and family by providing what is needful now, but also what may be needed at a later time. He also strengthens his family with love. He fills their hearts with hope and the desire to look out for each other.

To be strong in order to succor the weak and help them to become strong again.

To always be there for each other.

To always have enough to share with those outside their family who are in need.

Strength in a family comes from being true to the principles they have been taught and embraced. That family will be able to withstand any trial that comes their way and be even stronger as a result. Look for ways to strengthen your family from the inside out.

What are the strengths of your family?

_____

_____

_____

_____

Steps to Take to Return Home

How could you be stronger?

___

___

___

___

Gerard

★ ★ ★

Forgiveness is a secret weapon. A weapon in the battle for love. The first thing that comes to your mind might be the dialogue, "I am sorry, please forgive me," with the hope that you will be forgiven for whatever you did or didn't do, whatever you said or didn't say. You might think of the sorrow that is attached to someone who knows they have wronged someone and feels the wedge it has caused in their relationship.

The person granting the forgiveness seems to hold eternity in that moment. If they choose to forgive, hearts and lives can be mended. If they don't forgive, relationships fall apart, and the wedge grows along with the burden both parties carry for the rest of their lives.

To forgive requires a soft heart full of love, trust and a desire to be rid of the burden they carry of hurt, betrayal or broken promises. I hope you have a soft heart when the time comes.

Who do you need to forgive?

___

___

Sandy

★ ✹ ★

Time is a finite commodity. How you use your time will determine what you leave this earth with. Will you use it in your search for pleasure? For self-gratification? For things that bring you happiness? For things that bring others happiness? What you spend your time doing makes you better at it. No matter what it is. Do you ever say, "I wish I had more time for _____?"

It is human nature to make time for the things that are most important to you. Are you making time for those most important things?

What are your most important things?

Percy

★ ✹ ★

Whose responsibility is it? This is a question that deserves some thought.

Who is responsible for your happiness, your attitude, and your growth? What happens when you defer that responsibility to someone else? In a specific situation can you differentiate between your responsibility and that of others? Taking responsibility for your actions, for your success and failures is essential for your growth and happiness. Abdicating your responsibility onto others does everyone a disservice.

Accepting our responsibility in certain circumstances can take courage and a large measure of humility. But it helps make everyone involved a bit stronger as a result. Your family, your workplaces, your society would be better places if people took their responsibilities more seriously and embraced them freely.

Be responsible for your actions and make the world a little better.

Charity

What are you generous with? Your time, your talents, your money, your smiles, your faith? What are you stingy with?

Generosity is a mindset that says there is enough for everyone and that I don't need to worry if I give or share what I have. I will be compensated somehow. It may not be with the thing or item I gave or shared, but it will come back to me. Not knowing what will come of my generosity allows me to give and share freely without strings or expectations.

The more that you are generous in your daily walk and talk, the more you will receive. If there are some areas of your life you find it hard to give and share, it might be worth your time and energy to find out why. Resolve it.

Allow generosity to bless and improve that specific area of your life. You can never go wrong being generous, for the right reasons, at the right time, and in the right circumstances.

Stephanie

A wise man said, "as a man thinketh in his heart so is he." You might wonder how you can "think" in your heart? Does the heart have the ability to think? The statement implies there is a connection between your heart and your brain, as well as the possibility that your heart can influence your brain and your thinking.

Does that mean your thoughts make you who you are? I believe they do. So you might want to check and see what aspects of your life you want to change, determine what thoughts are fueling those aspects, and change your thoughts. If you need help, ask for it, look for it, and expect it to materialize. Then watch for the changes and miracles to take place and your life to improve as you become the person you can be.

Samantha

Have you ever considered your future? If you have, have you identified what you would like your future to look like?

_____

_____

Steps to Take to Return Home

_____

_____

If you have identified what your future looks like, what are the specific action items you have put in place to accomplish your plans for your future?

_____

_____

_____

_____

What happens if you don't plan and take action? Life goes on and you are at the mercy of someone else's plans. Not to plan is tantamount to turning your life over to someone else or something else and ending up, at the end of your journey, with regrets and failed dreams.

So, where do you start? Take time to think about what legacy you want to leave behind, the experiences you want to have, and who you want to have those experiences with.

_____

_____

_____

_____

Then ponder and think on what it will take to accomplish your desires. Break those things down into smaller, doable pieces. Once you have all that worked out, make a list of action items that you can sustain.

_____

_____

_____

_____

If you get overwhelmed, no progress will be made. Be patient. Be kind to yourself. Enlist the help of others. Keep adapting to your eventual successes along the way. Celebrate what you accomplish and rest easy knowing your dreams and desires are becoming reality.

Herbert

Serendipity is defined as unexpected opportunities that present themselves in your life that you can act on or ignore. It may be an answer to a prayer or a question that comes packaged in a way you weren't expecting. They are like little presents from heaven just for you.

Gladys

There is something powerful about being in a state of stillness. Stillness opens doors that are unavailable to you in your busy life. Even when you are asleep your mind isn't still. When you still your mind you make space available for answers you are seeking. You can connect to the wisdom of the universe. One of the benefits of stillness is giving your thought processes a much-needed break. Your whole body will benefit from connecting with this place of stillness. There are many ways to accomplish this. You might know someone that meditates successfully. You can try to do what they do to get the results that they get. Just find the ways that work for you and start experiencing the benefits.

Chandler

You leave a little bit of yourself everywhere you go. The presence you share with others, the facial expressions, the words and even your thoughts, affect the people you encounter. Whomever you come in contact with affects you as well. Some of this you are conscience of and much of it you probably don't see but you feel it.

Do you have any control over what you share or project onto others or what is projected or shared with you? Yes, you do. The first step is becoming aware of what is happening when it happens. Then determine if it is something that you want to happen or something you would like to change for the better.

You can control your thoughts. The thoughts you aren't aware of and can't identify are the harder ones to change. Be aware of how people react to you and how you react to them. Make the necessary changes in yourself if you want to improve how you present yourself and the message you want to share with the world.

Geena

Unconditional love is a precious quality to have and to receive. It is love with no conditions. It is uncomplicated and pure. To love someone unconditionally is to give a gift that surpasses any other gift they can receive. And it is the same for those that receive it. It doesn't mean that everything is perfect between whomever is giving and receiving that love. To be able to love with this love is something to strive for. Its companions are humility, sacrifice, and compassion, among others.

When you seek for the ability to have this kind of love for yourself and others, your world will expand in ways you couldn't even imagine.

Sarah

All around you, through you, and in you is a substance that connects you to everything. It transcends time and space. It is a place where you can go to ask questions, receive answers and feel love, light, and peace. Healing is woven in and through all of it. This is where stillness comes in. As you become more comfortable and familiar with stillness, more will become available to you. Be prepared for truth and knowledge to be shown you. This takes work, patience, perseverance and trust. Be brave.

Collin

Just breathe. How many times have you been told that? Try a little experiment. Next time you start to feel anxious or worried, take a few slow deep breaths and feel the tension in your body dissipate. Do it a big longer if you need to. Your mind and thoughts will slow down too. Clarity will return and you will be able to see the truth more clearly. Trust the breath of life to calm you down and help you be more present in the moment. Take time to breathe in fresh clean air when you can. Send gratitude to your lungs and their making it possible for you to receive this breath of life.

Leonard

There is a flow to life that needs movement to remain healthy. When that flow stops, stagnation happens and things die.

Your blood flows. There are many rhythms in your body and energy that flow in cycles and circuits. Water flows. The earth moves in an orbit and a rotation. Tides ebb and flow.

Growing in nature is movement. Built into that growth is a stopping point where death occurs. But even then, the flow of life recycles what is dead and new life begins. There are many examples of the flow of life. The trouble starts when that flow is impeded, cut off, or blocked.

You were meant to flow, to grow, to expand, and to move. Look for ways to clear whatever is impeding your flow.

Alonzo

The heart has many descriptors. Soft, hard, bleeding, big, cold, merry, open, kind, and more. What does a soft heart feel like? It feels compassion, love, kindness, sympathy, patience and is teachable. A hard heart is unreachable, closed off, unkind, unfeeling and impenetrable.

When truth is presented to a soft heart there is learning and acceptance. When truth is presented to a hard heart there is resistance, rejection, and sometimes retaliation.

Do a checkup and evaluate what kind of heart you have. You might want to make some improvements so truth can bring you closer to a state of joy and happiness. Because that is where a soft heart dwells.

How would you describe your heart?

_____

_____

_____

_____

Pomeroy

A champion is one who has been victorious, who has excelled beyond the performances of all others. A champion is one who has overcome obstacles, beat the odds, and proven the naysayers wrong. Life is like a championship, only it is with yourself that you are competing. To be victorious over all that would stop you from progressing to the finish line.

Some of those obstacles come because of others but most of them you put there, not meaning to. Obstacles like doubt, distraction, lack of commitment, listening to others tell you it's not possible, and not keeping your eyes on the goal.

To be your champion you need a clearly defined goal.

Steps to Take to Return Home

You need to be completely committed to that goal and willing to do whatever it takes to achieve it.

Along the way you need to be willing to share what you learn and your little successes to others coming behind you because they need a helping hand.

Keep your goal in sight.

Pick yourself back up and keep going when you get distracted or discouraged.

Only you can do this for yourself.

Be brave.

Be determined.

When you get there, the sweetness will be indescribable. The celebration when you get there will be otherworldly.

Charlotte

Write your feelings down. Keep a record of your journey. Reference it often so you don't forget what it took to achieve what you have accomplished. Write the truth. Write from your heart. Celebrate your successes even if they are small and may seem insignificant to someone else. Celebrate the magnificence of you, of who you are now and who you are becoming. Look forward to better days, better relationships, and more joy and happiness. Keep your heart soft and your eyes and ears open. Namaste.

Linda

NOTES

Chapter 9

Who Are You Now?

You have learned some new things and become aware of other things you may have forgotten. Hopefully these things spurred you to make some changes for the better. The process may have been painful or difficult but should have been rewarding enough to continue discovering more about who you are and who you are becoming.

The important thing is to keep discovering, learning, and moving in a positive direction.

All that being said, let's check in on where you're at right now.

Sarah

Evaluate where you are today. Record where you want to be and break that down into daily, weekly, and monthly goals. Use the charts provided on the following pages to track your progress if that helps you stay focused and committed.

Madeline

FOR YOU: A Guide to the Universe

PHYSICAL	Now	Goal
Water		
Diet		
Activity		
Nature		
Skin		
Eyes		
Sleep		
Physical check-up		

Who Are You Now?

SPIRITUAL	Now	Goal
Prayer		
Reading		
Stillness		
Meditation		
Worship		

Parker

PSYCHOLOGICAL	Now	Goal
Knowledge/ learning		
Stress/ability to cope with life		

Seek professional help when needed.

Portense

Start with the relationship that is the most important. Determine what you want from the relationship and then define your intentions. Decide what you are willing to give. Establish any boundaries that may be needed.

RELATIONSHIPS	Now	Goal
Between yourself		
God		
Partner/spouse		
Children		
Parents		
Immediate family		
Extended family		

Co-workers		
Friends		
Neighbors		
Animals		
Nature		

Simon

In the chart below list the emotions you don't want to keep, such as anger, doubt, fear, jealousy, or hopelessness; and emotions you want to cultivate, such as joy or hope.

EMOTIONAL

Emotions I don't want to keep	Emotions I want to strengthen

Seek someone's help if you don't know what to do. Once you are on the right track for the emotion you have been working on, then go onto the next one. This is a continuous process of changing upward.

Peter

The blank worksheets on the following pages are provided for you to use or copy as needed so you can individualize and track any of the goals you have decided to work on.

GOAL WORKSHEET

MY GOAL: _____

Start date: _____

Target completion date: _____

Steps to reach my goal:

1. _____
   _____
   _____

2. _____
   _____
   _____

3. _____
   _____
   _____

4. _____
   _____
   _____

5. _____
   _____
   _____

6. _____
   _____
   _____

Date completed: _____

FOR YOU: A Guide to the Universe

GOAL WORKSHEET

MY GOAL: _____

Start date: _____

Target completion date: _____

Steps to reach my goal:

1. _____
_____
_____

2. _____
_____
_____

3. _____
_____
_____

4. _____
_____
_____

5. _____
_____
_____

6. _____
_____
_____

Date completed: _____

Chapter 10

What Do You Do Now?

It has been said that a well-lived life is a life well lived. To live well the life you've been given, is something you need to work at every day. This takes thought, planning, and action on your part. Everything you need, to have no regrets when your life comes to an end, is available to you now. It will take seeking and asking, giving and taking. The days ahead are going to put you to the test. Courage and strength will serve you well.

I have seen your day. I know what is coming. Please don't wait. The strong will survive. Do what you need to do now. There are heavenly hosts praying for you and people on earth ready to help and support you. You were meant for this time and this place.

William

Never ever forget who you are: a child of your Heavenly Father who loves you. You are worth fighting for. You have an important purpose here.

If you doubt that, ask God what He thinks about you and write down what He says.

_____

_____

_____

_____

Mitch

What if you are broken? What if you are so far gone you don't think there is any way back? What if you have done terrible things or been a terrible person?

You are still loved. There is still hope. There is always a way back. The fact that you have made it through the book to these last pages means you can do this, you want to do this, and you can come back to light, love, and peace.

You know what you need to do to bring light into your life. Deep inside you is the warmth you read about. Let it help you move the darkness out.

Reread the parts of the book that gave you hope and courage.

Be patient and forgiving of yourself and others.

Don't give up.

Support people will come into your life right when you need them. Allow their love and compassion to envelop you and connect you to the light and warmth in you.

I'm sending you light. Can you feel it?

Let it in. Let it warm you until you can connect to the light that surrounds you.

What Do You Do Now?

Don't give up.

Tim

For those of you who have some light in your life I hope you have had some questions answered, some "aha" moments, and want to know more.

Ask to know if the words contained within these pages are truth. Don't take our word for it. Find out for yourself. Write your experiences down. Use your experiences to help others find answers to their questions.

No matter what is happening around you or in the world, it is never too late to find out who you truly are and to become the person you were meant to be.

Solomon

So, we come to the end of this book, but not your journey. There is so much more to come.

There will come a day when everyone on earth will know the truth: the truth about themselves, about God, and about what's next. Even then, you will have the choice to believe, or not.

So, if you already know who you truly are and are living as your true self, help others do the same. If you want to know your true self, embrace and receive the truths in the pages of this book. It was written *for you*.

Tunis

NOTES

What Do You Do Now?

NOTES

NOTES

Made in the USA
Middletown, DE
13 February 2022